CHARLES W. CHESNUTT

A Study of the Short Fiction

Twayne publishes studies of all major short-story writers worldwide. For a complete list, contact the Publisher directly.

Twayne's Studies in Short Fiction

Gary Scharnhorst and Eric Haralson,
General Editors

CHARLES W. CHESNUTT.
Cleveland Public Library Photograph Collection.

CHARLES W. CHESNUTT

A Study of the Short Fiction

Henry B. Wonham
University of Oregon

TWAYNE PUBLISHERS
An Imprint of Simon & Schuster Macmillan
New York

PRENTICE HALL INTERNATIONAL
London Mexico City New Delhi Singapore Sydney Toronto

Twayne's Studies in Short Fiction, No. 72

Twayne Publishers
An Imprint of Simon & Schuster Macmillan
1633 Broadway
New York, NY 10019

Library of Congress Cataloging-in-Publication Data

Wonham, Henry B., 1960–
    Charles W. Chesnutt : a study of the short fiction / Henry B. Wonham.
        p.   cm. — (Twayne's studies in short fiction ; no. 72)
    Includes bibliographical references and index.
    ISBN 0-8057-0869-3 (hard)
    1. Chesnutt, Charles Waddell, 1858–1932—Criticism and interpretation.   2. Afro-Americans in literature.   3. Short story.
I. Title.   II. Series.
PS1292.C6Z595   1998
813'.4—dc21   97-36416
                                                                      CIP

This paper meets the requirements of ANSI/NISO Z3948–1992 (Permanence of Paper).

10 9 8 7 6 5 4 3 2 1

Printed in the United States of America

For Henry Grant Wonham

Contents

Preface

This book offers a broad introduction to the short fiction of Charles W. Chesnutt. Assessing his achievement in 1900, one year after the prestigious firm of Houghton Mifflin had published *The Conjure Woman* and *The Wife of His Youth and Other Stories of the Color Line,* William Dean Howells compared Chesnutt with the acknowledged European masters of the genre, including Maupassant and Tourguenief. Chesnutt's dialect tales and postwar urban dramas, according to Howells, would appeal to "the more intelligent public" as evidence of a quiet artistry, comparable to that of better-known American contemporaries such as Henry James, Sarah Orne Jewett, and Mary Wilkins Freeman. Noting that in art "there is, happily, no color line," Howells affirmed that nothing could stop Chesnutt from someday occupying "one of the places at the top" of the literary pantheon, his special aptitude for short fiction sure to distinguish him "in a department of literature where Americans hold the foremost place."

The "more intelligent public" did not embrace Chesnutt as Howells had predicted, however, and his reputation as a master of the short story has only recently begun to recover the stature Howells briefly bestowed. After years of obscurity and neglect, Chesnutt has made a stunning comeback, and the impressive volume of commentary suddenly devoted to his writing has tended to validate Howells's lofty comparative choices, even while exposing the idealistic basis for his assessment. As every triumph and every defeat in Chesnutt's short literary career testifies, the color line extends well into the aesthetic field, and its influence over the production and reception of literary works at the turn of the century can hardly be overestimated. Indeed, the dramatic surge in Chesnutt studies can be attributed to the fact that he explored the causes and effects of this pervasive influence more subtly and creatively than any of his contemporaries, black or white. In adding another voice to the burgeoning critical discussion of his work, I have attempted little more than to elaborate and substantiate Howells's high opinion of Chesnutt's achievement as a writer of short fiction, while reassessing the racially charged assumptions upon which that opinion rests. The "more intelligent public" today, it seems, is prepared to appreciate the masterful tales of *The Conjure Woman* and *The Wife of His Youth* for many of the same qualities that Chesnutt's own contemporaries felt it necessary to excuse.

I would like to thank Gary Scharnhorst and Eric Haralson for their editorial prowess and trusting hands-off approach to the management of this project, which has entitled me to so many hours of pleasure and so few of pain. I would also like to thank William Andrews for his generous advice and for the important standard his scholarship has set for Chesnutt studies. I received very helpful suggestions as well from Robert Nowatzki, whose dissertation convinced me that the future is bright for Chesnutt scholarship, whatever the present may reveal. The librarians at Fisk University, where the Chesnutt papers are held, have been extremely accommodating, as have my colleagues at the University of Oregon, who provided the time and resources necessary to complete the manuscript. Finally, I would like to thank the most important people in my life, Connie and Emory Wonham, for their constant love and support, and Henry Grant Wonham, who did everything in his power to see that this book would never be finished, and to whom it is lovingly dedicated.

Acknowledgments

The following publishers granted permission to reprint copyrighted material: Louisiana State University Press for William L. Andrews's *The Literary Career of Charles W. Chesnutt;* University of Chicago Press for Houston A. Baker Jr.'s *Modernism and the Harlem Renaissance;* Harvard University Press for Eric J. Sundquist's *To Wake the Nations: Race in the Making of American Literature;* Oxford University Press and *American Literary History* for Ben Slote's "Listening to 'The Goophered Grapevine' and Hearing Raisins Sing."

Part 1

THE SHORT FICTION

Introduction

One of the many arresting ironies of Charles W. Chesnutt's brilliant but abbreviated literary career lies in the fact that the masterful short stories for which he will be remembered in anthologies and histories of American literature were intended as preparation. Chesnutt's grandiose literary ambitions always pointed in the direction of the novel, the one form through which he felt it might be possible to earn the financial rewards and the widespread notoriety he so earnestly desired. "I want fame; I want money," he confided to his journal in 1881; "I want to raise my children in a different rank of life from that I sprang from."[1] As the 23-year-old principal of the State Colored Normal School in Fayetteville, North Carolina, he worried that he "would never accumulate a competency," and he bridled at the prospect of a long professional apprenticeship in law or medicine. "But literature pays," he wrote hopefully, adding an all-important qualifier, after a pause, "—the successful" (*Journals*, 154). By "the successful," Chesnutt had in mind the leading popular novelists of his day: Harriet Beecher Stowe, Albion Tourgée, Mark Twain, and George Washington Cable, among others. In the same 1881 journal entry he exclaimed, "It is the dream of my life—to be an author," and he went on to describe the significant shape of another "successful" writer's career: "I have just finished Thackeray's 'Vanity Fair,' his first great novel. He had written much previous to its appearance, but with 'Vanity Fair' he made himself a reputation" (*Journals*, 154). Apprentice work in short fiction might do for the moment, he consoled himself, but his highest ambition was to forge a reputation as a novelist, perhaps even to write a "better book about the South than Judge Tourgée or Mrs. Stowe has written?" (*Journals*, 125).

Despite his persistent belief that the novel necessarily constituted the nineteenth-century writer's crowning achievement, Chesnutt never wrote a *Vanity Fair* or an *Uncle Tom's Cabin*, nor did he even come close to matching the popular success of Tourgée's *A Fool's Errand*. His three published novels, *The House Behind the Cedars* (1900), *The Marrow of Tradition* (1901), and *The Colonel's Dream* (1905), all provide fascinating representations of post-Reconstruction American life, but none possesses the lyrical intensity, pathos, and humor of Chesnutt's best short stories. Indeed, by his own measure, Chesnutt's brief literary career produced more disappointment than success, for with the stories he composed throughout the 1880s and '90s, he intended to strike "an entering wedge in the literary world," which he could "drive in further afterwards" (*Journals*, 155). This "entering wedge" never culminated in the sort of novelistic success he envisioned for himself, but Chesnutt's work of preparation, the two short-story collections published in 1899 as *The Conjure Woman* and *The Wife of His Youth*, undeniably constitute a major literary achievement in their own right, a body of work worthy of comparison with the finest American short fiction.

Chesnutt's awkward straddling of the generic boundary between the novel and short story is nowhere more keenly apparent than in his 10-year struggle with the manuscript of "Rena Walden," arguably his most important short story.[2] "Rena" originated in 1889 as a tale of life along the color line, sympathetically chronicling the destructive effects of racial prejudice upon the aspirations of a mixed-race Southern family. Chesnutt was devastated when Richard Watson Gilder of the *Century Magazine* rejected the story on the grounds that its mixed-race characters were "unnatural" and the story's sentiment "amorphous."[3] In an angry letter to his friend and advisor George Washington Cable, Chesnutt vented his rage at the short-story conventions that informed Gilder's comments, expressing his disdain for the standard magazine representation of African Americans as devoted servants whose "chief virtues have been their dog-like fidelity to their old master" (Helen Chesnutt, 57). The leading practitioners of the "plantation tradition" in American fiction, including such writers as Thomas Nelson Page and Thomas Dixon, had excelled at sentimentalizing the old-time negro as a character who, according to Chesnutt's apt assessment, "prefers kicks to half-pence."[4] "Such characters exist," he impatiently admitted, "but I can't write about those people, or rather I won't write about them" (Helen Chesnutt, 57–58).

Gilder's comments helped to confirm Chesnutt's suspicion that magazines such as the *Century*, *Harpers New Monthly Magazine*, and the *Atlantic Monthly*, the major forums for short-story publication in America, were unprepared for a sympathetic representation of literate "mulatto" culture, which Gilder had so tellingly deemed "unnatural" and which the reading public seemed all too ready to dismiss as, in Chesnutt's words,

"an insult to nature" (Helen Chesnutt, 57). Moreover, Gilder's deference to popular taste in the literary portrayal of African Americans carried with it a brutally personal affront, for at the time of its composition
"Rena Walden" constituted Chesnutt's most concentrated attempt to
address his own complicated racial identity in fiction. Thus rather than
abandon the story after its rejection, he spent nearly a decade reworking
his tale of postwar Southern life into what he believed would be the
more suitable form of a novel, which he submitted to Houghton Mifflin
in 1899. The prestigious firm's rejection of the manuscript in March of
that year came as another devastating blow, made only more puzzling by
Walter Hines Page's consoling explanation, written on behalf of
Houghton Mifflin:

> I feel, I think, as badly as you do about Rena.... The feeling here was,
> and to some extent at least I share it, that you had so long and so suc-
> cessfully accustomed yourself to the construction of short stories that
> you have not yet, so to speak, got away from the short story measure-
> ment and the short story habit. (Helen Chesnutt, 109)

Rejected by the *Century* for his failure to deploy the stock conventions
of the magazine short story, snubbed by Houghton Mifflin for his failure
to break the habit of short-story composition, Chesnutt in 1899 found
his most cherished manuscript suspended in a generic double-bind.
"Rena Walden" did finally appear in print a year later when Walter Hines
Page agreed to publish the novel after yet another set of revisions under
the title *The House Behind the Cedars,* but the decade-long struggle to find
a form for the story had clearly tempered Chesnutt's sense of achievement at having finally, at age 42, produced his first novel. He continued
to regard short fiction as preparation for his own imminent *Vanity Fair,*
the really important novelistic work that would make his reputation,
but "Rena" 's troubled evolution from a short story into a novel betrayed
the complexity of Chesnutt's relationship to a literary establishment
presided over by men like Gilder and Page. As he already knew all too
well, effective resistance to the dominant forms of nineteenth-century
American fiction, especially in the domain of racial characterization,
required subtlety and indirection. "The almost indefinable feeling of
repulsion toward the negro ... cannot be stormed or taken by assault,"
he had written in 1880, long before cultivating the literary resources
necessary to engage in such resistance. "The garrison will not capitu-

late: so their position must be mined, and we will find ourselves in their midst before they think it" (*Journals*, 140). For all Chesnutt's desire to distinguish himself as a novelist, this conception of literary work as a form of cultural espionage imposed unique creative pressures on his art, pressures to which he responded most effectively not with the great popular novel he longed to write but with a brilliant array of aesthetic compromises that produced his most distinctive short fiction.

Chesnutt had excellent reasons for taking "Rena Walden" 's plight personally (he admitted in a letter to Page, "I have not slept with that story for ten years without falling in love with it"), for he was no stranger to the paralyzing experience of "Rena" 's double-bind (Helen Chesnutt, 108). As the son of free black parents, both of whom possessed white ancestry, he grew up in the intensely color-conscious atmosphere of Reconstruction North Carolina, where Ann Maria and Andrew Jackson Chesnutt had relocated immediately after the Civil War. His white grandfather, Waddell Cade, a Fayetteville tobacco merchant, had assisted in supporting the five illegitimate children he sired with Ann Chesnutt, his housekeeper, but Cade never acknowledged his paternity, and many years later Charles Chesnutt still wrangled uncomfortably with the twin cultural stigmas of illegitimacy and miscegenation. After the war, Chesnutt's parents became leading members of Fayetteville's small but vibrant black middle class, and he indulged his bookish nature by taking full advantage of the unprecedented educational opportunities made available during Reconstruction by the Freedman's Bureau.

His meteoric academic progress, accomplished largely through a rigorous program of self-study, culminated in 1880 with Chesnutt's appointment as principal of the State Colored Normal School, the only institution of its kind in North Carolina, but already at age 22 his ambitions had begun to focus beyond Fayetteville. His marriage to Susan Perry two years earlier, in 1878, had introduced the prospect of raising his own children in the deteriorating racial climate of post-Reconstruction North Carolina. This unsettling thought, coupled with his persistent dream "to be an author," compelled Chesnutt to begin searching for a Northern berth, where he might "get employment in some literary avocation, or something leading in that direction" (*Journals*, 106). Flexible as his plans remained, he had clearly begun to sense the impossibility of his present situation, later to be powerfully dramatized in tales of plantation life and stories of the color line, but here registered in the frustrated private tones of his journal:

I occupy here a position similar to that of the Mahomet's Coffin. I am neither fish[,] flesh, nor fowl neither "nigger", poor white, nor "buckrah." Too "stuck up" for the colored folks, and, of course, not recognized by the whites. Now these things I would imagine I would escape from, in some degree, if I lived in the North. The Colored people would be more intelligent, and the white people less prejudiced; so that if I did not reach *terra firma*, I would at least be in sight of land. (*Journals*, 157–58)

In 1883, Chesnutt decided to try his fortunes in New York City, where he established himself briefly as a Dow Jones reporter and stenographer, before moving on to the city of his birth, Cleveland, Ohio. With awesome industry and self-discipline, he proceeded to carve out a successful business in stenography while somehow finding the time to undertake a course in legal studies and, in the few hours that remained his own, to begin composing sentimental and comic sketches for publication. In 1887 he simultaneously passed the Ohio bar exam and broke into the elite rank of American writers by publishing "The Goophered Grapevine" in the nation's leading literary periodical, the *Atlantic Monthly*. The widespread acclaim that greeted this conjure tale about plantation life "befo' de wah" inspired two more contributions to the *Atlantic*, including the conjure tale "Po' Sandy" and a dialect story, "Dave's Neckliss," in which, as he later explained, Chesnutt attempted for the first time "to get out of realm of superstition [and] into the realm of feeling and passion" (Andrews, 21).

In all three stories Chesnutt had shrewdly deployed the plantation tradition for his own decidedly unsentimental purposes, but by 1889 he was already determined to distance himself from the nostalgic mood and the stock characterizations of the plantation formula. "I think I have about used up the old Negro who serves as mouthpiece," he informed Tourgée, "and I shall drop him in future stories, as well as much of the dialect" (Andrews, 21). The problematic "Rena Walden" manuscript was one result of this shift in style and emphasis away from the plantation dialect tale and toward a more "realistic" representation of postwar Southern economic and social conditions. While "Rena" underwent the prolonged scrutiny of several recalcitrant editors, including Gilder and Page, Chesnutt had more success with "The Sheriff's Children," his first important nondialect story, which appeared in the New York *Independent* in 1889.

He continued to write in the nondialect vein throughout the 1890s, expanding "Rena Walden" and devoting his apparently limitless energies to two other novel manuscripts as well, "Mandy Oxendine" and "A Business Career," both of which were ultimately rejected for publication. Still smarting from the first of these disappointments in October 1897, Chesnutt approached Houghton Mifflin about the possibility of compiling a book out of his strongest short stories.[5] The firm agreed to consider the idea but responded in March of the following year with the unpleasant news that it could offer to publish neither the story collection nor the second novel manuscript, "A Business Career," which constituted in its view "a doubtful venture" (Helen Chesnutt, 91). Again writing to console the disappointed author on behalf of Houghton Mifflin, Walter Hines Page hinted that if Chesnutt could return to the conjure tales of plantation life, of which he had written only three before abandoning "the realm of superstition," then the firm might be willing to reconsider its decision. Chesnutt had deliberately left the plantation formula behind in favor of what he considered his more probing nondialect tales of racial strife and moral compromise, including stories like "The Wife of His Youth," which earned critical acclaim when it appeared in the July 1898 *Atlantic Monthly*, but he also earnestly desired to publish a book. Thus he accepted Page's terms and, with characteristic dispatch, composed six new conjure stories almost immediately. Page supplied a title, *The Conjure Woman*, and presided over the final winnowing of the collection, which ultimately included seven dialect tales narrated by the ex-slave Uncle Julius. The volume appeared in March 1899.

Critics had barely begun to weigh in with enthusiastic reviews of *The Conjure Woman* when Chesnutt began lobbying Houghton Mifflin about a follow-up collection intended to feature his nondialect writing. While the firm again deliberated over his work, including several of the same stories recently rejected for book publication, public interest in the author grew rapidly, and speculation about his racial identity became widespread. In his initial correspondence with Houghton Mifflin in 1891, Chesnutt had described himself as "an American of acknowledged African descent," but throughout the 1890s he had elected not to advertise his lineage as a literary credential, preferring to allow his tales to play ambivalently with and against public assumptions (Helen Chesnutt, 68–69).[6] His decision to remain silent about his racial identity rested on complex aesthetic and practical considerations, but by the summer of 1899 both he and Houghton Mifflin could appreciate the marketing and publicity advantages of a full disclosure. News of the author's "African descent" thus traveled quickly that summer amid general critical approval of *The Conjure Woman,* and by August 1899 Houghton Mifflin had agreed to produce a new collection of his stories. Poised to capitalize on Chesnutt's potential appeal to African-American as well as white readers, his publishers were careful to issue *The Wife of His Youth and Other Stories of the Color Line* (the title again supplied by Page) in time for the Christmas season.

Chesnutt's reputation as a writer of short fiction rests almost exclusively on his achievement in these two undeniably haphazard publishing ventures. William Andrews, Chesnutt's foremost academic critic, claims that *The Wife of His Youth,* "like its predecessor, *The Conjure Woman,* evolved more as a by-product of its author's scattered labors in the short story than as the purposefully planned outcome of a phase of his literary development" (Andrews, 37). This unavoidable insight is meant not to belittle Chesnutt's major achievement in the art of the short story but rather to characterize that achievement by alluding again to his ambivalent relation to the genre. With his multiple offerings in the 1899 book market, Chesnutt felt he had finally achieved the "entering wedge in the literary world" that would initiate his novelistic success. To that end, he closed his lucrative stenography business in the fall of 1899 and began to pursue his dream in earnest, publishing *The House Behind the Cedars* in 1900 and the novel Andrews calls Chesnutt's magnum opus, *The Marrow of Tradition,* the following year (Andrews, 175). Thus after achieving considerable notoriety as a writer of short stories by 1899, Chesnutt promptly abandoned the form, returning to it only briefly in late 1903, when his flagging novelistic reputation needed a boost.

His return to the form that had made him famous was, like Chesnutt's literary career more generally, brief but spectacular. For all its power and scope, *The Marrow of Tradition* had impressed many critics as an overly bitter and propagandistic appeal for racial justice, and Chesnutt's confidence in his ability to write a popular novel of purpose was clearly shaken. As in the past when his overt social criticism had been attacked or simply rejected, he resorted to a quieter pitch, framing his drama of resistance within the neatly concentrated space of the short story. "Baxter's Procrustes," Chesnutt's most polished indictment of racial bias within the literary establishment, appeared in the *Atlantic Monthly* in 1904 and marked the end of his nearly five-year commitment to full-time authorship. His formal abandonment of the boyhood dream would not come until the following year, when lukewarm reviews of his last published novel, *The Colonel's Dream,* consolidated his frustration, but the decision had been looming for some time, and the ironic detachment of Chesnutt's hero in "Baxter's Procrustes" had clearly anticipated a shift in professional orientation. Financial pressures had already compelled him to take up stenography again in 1902, and three years later he was ready to devote himself entirely to business.

Chesnutt continued after 1905 to "tinker with the materials of his art," as Andrews puts it, but he never duplicated either the passion of *The Marrow of Tradition* or the subtle humor of "Baxter's Procrustes" (Andrews, 261). His career had, in a sense, climaxed with the "entering wedge" that marked its official beginning in 1899, the year that produced both *The Conjure Woman* and *The Wife of His Youth*. The awkward shape of Chesnutt's career must not, however, be interpreted as a token of his artistic failure. If Chesnutt failed in anything, it was in his effort to structure a literary career according to conventional models that simply did not apply to his unique standing in relation to the American literary establishment.[7] The complexity of this relation demanded a subtle artistry of indirection and compromise, which he never thoroughly transported to the literary genre that meant the most to him, the novel of purpose. However little he may have valued his achievement in a more minor key, Chesnutt's true genius for giving linguistic form to the racial dynamics of the era he named "Post-Bellum—Pre-Harlem" emerges most clearly and memorably in his short fiction.

The Dialect Tales

"The Goophered Grapevine"

Chesnutt arrived suddenly on the national literary scene in August 1887
with the appearance of "The Goophered Grapevine" in the auspicious
pages of the *Atlantic Monthly*. As his most frequently anthologized work,
and as the tale Chesnutt selected to open his first collection of stories,
"The Goophered Grapevine" continues to function for most readers as
an introduction to the fictional plantation world of *The Conjure Woman*, a
world inhabited by ex-slaves, disinherited Southerners, and acquisitive
Yankees. In their complex maneuvering for authority within the realm of
Chesnutt's postwar Southern plantation, these figures resort to every
available means of influencing the social and economic conditions under
which they live and work together. For Uncle Julius, the personality
around whom the tales of *The Conjure Woman* revolve, the key to maintaining some measure of authority in the uncertain postwar era lies in
his imaginative reconstruction of the slave past, his ability to control
and manipulate the legacy of slavery to his own advantage. Thus in
"The Goophered Grapevine" and in each of the succeeding tales of *The
Conjure Woman*, storytelling functions for Uncle Julius, and for Chesnutt
himself, as a means of creative resistance to forces threatening to compromise the hard-earned liberties of African Americans in the years after
Reconstruction.

Of course, Uncle Julius's adversarial relation to these forces, embodied most comprehensively in the economic "improvements" initiated by
the Ohioan John, is carefully guarded. Indeed, for most readers of the
Atlantic Monthly's August 1887 issue, the designation "uncle," when
applied to a black man, invoked a broad set of cultural assumptions that
suggested anything but resistance. By the end of Reconstruction, the
Christlike image of Harriet Beecher Stowe's abolitionist icon, Uncle
Tom, had spawned a generation of postwar ante-types, including Joel
Chandler Harris's motherly Uncle Remus. This highly cultivated representation of African-American masculinity was so pervasively accepted

11

because it performed such essential cultural work, in effect obscuring black male potency to allay anxiety about a figure presumed to be inherently threatening to civilized norms, Chesnutt's choice of Uncle Julius, in John's words "a venerable-looking colored man," as the mouthpiece for the conjure tales thus involved a significant concession to the formal expectations of his mainly white audience; but, as always in Chesnutt's art, this concession made available a wealth of ironic possibilities through which the author's own literary conjure achieves its powerful effect of resistance.[8]

One need only consider the probable source for "The Goophered Grapevine," an actual folktale in which a slave's sexual prowess is linked to the grapevine's cyclical pattern of growth and decay, to appreciate the charged irony of Uncle Julius's performance in Chesnutt's first plantation story. The folktale reproduced in Robert Hemenway's pioneering essay, "The Functions of Folklore in Charles Chesnutt's *The Conjure Woman*," describes a slave who, after anointing his head every spring with sap from the grapevines, develops a reputation for "being able to bring the greatest sexual feelings possible."[9] Although in Julius's version it is the slave Henry's hair, and not his penis, that grows longer in springtime, this calculated alteration of the folk original only modifies the story's glaring challenge to the very assumptions about black male sexuality that Julius's familial sobriquet ostensibly serves to confirm.

To further obscure—and intensify—Julius's powers of narrative resistance, Chesnutt filters the ex-slave's oral performances through John's Northern eyes and ears, setting in motion a tense triangular drama of interpretation between Julius, John, and John's neurasthenic wife, Annie. In fact, while Julius's stories of plantation life call for explicit interpretive gestures from the Northern couple, his very appearance elicits its own complex set of responses. Upon first encountering Julius in "The Goophered Grapevine," for example, John unwittingly observes a carefully orchestrated image of African-American behavior, to which he confidently applies his own interpretive touches. John explains that Julius "held on his knees a hat full of grapes, over which he was smacking his lips with great gusto, and a pile of grapeskins near him indicated that the performance was no new thing. We approached him at an angle from the rear, and we were close to him before he perceived us. He respectfully rose as we drew near, and was moving away when I begged him to keep his seat" (*Conjure*, 34).

John regards Julius's lip-smacking gusto as a figurative "performance," but his assumption that he and Annie occupy a superior point of vantage—an assumption Julius subtly cultivates through gestures of respect and retreat—blinds John to his own role as an all-too-willing consumer of what is literally a minstrel performance. Impressed by the old man's demonstration of respect and conformity to stereotype, John notes the "embarrassment" with which Julius reluctantly agrees to transgress local custom by resuming his seat beside the white couple. "There is plenty of room for us all," insists the Northerner, who repeatedly demonstrates his skin-deep progessivism through such token acts of inclusion (*Conjure*, 34). As Julius understands, there may be enough room on the new Southern plantation for an old-time negro of the sort that, in Chesnutt's words, prefers "kicks to half-pence," but there is hardly enough room for two proprietors (Helen Chesnutt, 58). Thus after fielding the first of many questions John will eventually ask about local history, Julius interrupts with a question of his own, one that makes it unmistakably clear who has really approached whom at an angle from the rear: "Is you de Norv'n gemman w'at's gwine ter buy de ole vimya'd?" (*Conjure*, 34).

Despite this indication that he has seen John and Annie coming, and that he has considered the economic consequences to himself of John's proposed investment, Julius has very little leverage in the imminent confrontation over control of the vineyard. Thus it suits his purposes to resume the minstrel mask by dropping into a tale of plantation life "befo' de wah," adopting a "dreamy expression" that again deliberately concedes John's superior faculty of vision: "At first the current of his memory—or imagination—seemed somewhat sluggish; but as his embarrassment wore off, his language flowed more freely, and the story acquired perspective and coherence. As he became more and more absorbed in the narrative, his eyes assumed a dreamy expression, and he seemed to lose sight of his auditors, and to be living over again in monologue his life on the old plantation" (*Conjure*, 35). Contrary to John's self-serving impressions in this passage, Julius never loses sight of his Northern auditors, for whom this display of nostalgia is artfully feigned. Indeed, his tale opens with a catalog of stereotypical slave delicacies, tailored more for John's consumption than for the slaves who purportedly covet such foods: "Now, ef dey's an'thing a nigger lub, nex' ter 'possum, en chick'n, en watermillyums, it's scuppernon's. . . . W'en de season is nigh 'bout ober, en de grapes begin ter swivel up des a little wid de wrinkles er ole age,—w'en de skin git so sof' en brown,—den de scuppernon' make you smack yo' lip en roll yo' eye en wush fer mo' " (*Conjure*, 35–36). With this "somewhat sluggish" beginning, as John characterizes it, Julius has begun to construct a fictional antebellum world out of the stock materials of stage minstrelsy, going so far as to allude to the artifice of "blacking-up" with his reference to the seasonal discoloration of the grapes.[10] Such a characterization is undeniably demeaning to the very people for whom Julius apparently intends to generate sympathy, yet each of his self-effacing moves is part of a narrational strategy that Chesnutt deploys throughout *The Conjure Woman*, a strategy that begins with the storyteller's inhabitation of stereotype and ends with his assertion—often, it must be admitted, a distressingly ambivalent assertion—of the slave's humanity and of the freedman's dignity. Julius, in effect, disarms his listeners, just as Chesnutt intends to disarm his readers, by telling them what they already think they know, in order to divert attention from the more subtle content of his yarns, which typically disclose some aspect of the "intensely human" plight of African Americans before and after the war.[11]

In "The Goophered Grapevine" Julius crafts a tale about the fortunes of his former master, Ole Mars Dugal' McAdoo, "a monst'us keerless man," who anticipates the direction of the story by shooting himself in the leg in a vain effort to curtail the appetite of his slaves for the irresistible scuppernong grape (*Conjure*, 36). Frustrated by incessant raids on his vineyard, Mars Dugal' hires the local conjure woman, Aunt Peggy, to cast a spell over the vineyard that will intimidate his slaves and thus increase his yield. Peggy is seen the following day sauntering " 'roun' 'mongs' de vimes," performing her witchcraft in full view of the audience she hopes to influence (*Conjure*, 36). After rumors circulate about slaves who have died suddenly from eating the conjured grapes, Mars Dugal' enjoys an uncontested monopoly on the produce of his vines, until a "noo nigger" arrives on the plantation and unwittingly gorges himself on scuppernongs (*Conjure*, 37). To save himself, Henry, the afflicted slave, appeals to Aunt Peggy, who instructs him that each spring he must anoint his head with the sap of the scuppernong. He does so, but, as Julius relates: "de beatenes' thing you eber see happen ter Henry. Up ter dat time he wus ez ball ez a sweeten' 'tater, but des ez soon ez de young leaves begun ter come out on de grapevimes, de ha'r begun ter grow out on Henry's head, en by de middle er de summer he had de bigges' head er ha'r on de plantation" (*Conjure*, 39).

Not only does a seasonal crop of hair grow miraculously on Henry's head, but, as summer progresses, his hair "begun to quirl all up in little balls, des like dis yer reg'lar grapy ha'r, en by de time de grapes got ripe his head look des like a bunch er grapes" (*Conjure*, 39). In the fall, "when de sap begin ter go down in de grapevimes," Henry's hair falls out again, and his once "soopl en libely" body begins to suffer the effects of old age and chronic rheumatism (*Conjure*, 39). After the cycle has repeated itself often enough to have become predictable, Mars Dugal' recognizes an opportunity to cultivate his new cash crop by selling Henry for fifteen hundred dollars every spring, then offering to buy him back for five hundred in the fall, prompting Mars Dugal' to take "good keer uv 'im dyoin' er de winter," " 'caze a nigger w'at he could make a thousan' dollars a year off 'n didn' grow on eve'y huckleberry bush" (*Conjure*, 41).

The simultaneous demise of Henry and of the vines to which his fate has become tied occurs when Mars Dugal', having curbed the appetite of his slaves for the luscious scuppernong, yields to his own unlimited appetite for profit. In an effort to increase his income yet again, he invites a Yankee stranger to advise him on new techniques for cultivation of the crop, and, according to Julius, "Mars Dugal' des drunk it all in, des 'peared ter be bewitch' wid dat Yankee" (*Conjure*, 41). The fieldhands simply "shuk dere heads" when they saw the Yankee, like Aunt Peggy before him, "runnin' 'roun' de vimya'd en diggin' under de grapevimes," and later fixing up "a mixtry er lime en ashes en manyo" to pour around the roots of the vines (*Conjure*, 41). At first the vines flourish, but it soon turns out that the Yankee's conjuration has destroyed the vineyard, and as the last vine turns yellow and dies, "Henry died too— des went out sorter like a cannel.... The goopher had got de under holt, en th'owed Henry dat time fer good en all" (*Conjure*, 42). Julius concludes with a word of advice, addressing John with a title that reinforces the tale's implied analogy between antebellum and postbellum economic relations: "En I tell yer w'at, marster, I wouldn' 'vise you to buy dis yer ole vimya'd, 'caze de goopher's on it yet, en dey ain' no tellin' w'en it's gwine crap out" (*Conjure*, 43).

Julius's reasoning here demands scrutiny. His professed belief that Aunt Peggy's goopher has finally worked its fatal spell on Henry, and that the same goopher lingers ominously over the property, might be understood as a calculated effort to deflect John's attention from the really poignant content of the tale, its veiled parable about the disastrous consequences of Northern interference in Southern industries. Julius surely understands—and wishes to make John and Annie understand, if he can do so without challenging them directly—that it is the Yankee's meddling, with all that it subtly implies about John's intention to cultivate the property, that kills both Henry and the vines. But if the tale registers the human cost of Yankee economic imperialism, Julius has been careful to show that the substance of his threat, the legacy of Aunt Peggy's conjure, has traditionally accomplished nothing except to enrich the owner of the grapevine, and so his tale can hardly count as a disincentive to investment. In fact, when John eventually does purchase the vineyard, he harbors a "mild suspicion that our colored assistants do not suffer from a want of grapes," implying that the goopher is somewhat lacking in strength, according to his proprietary interests (*Conjure*, 43). To further problematize Julius's warning against investment in the plantation, John sensibly points out that, according to the tale, all the conjured vines died. Julius answers resourcefully: "Dey did 'pear ter die, but a few un 'em come out ag'in, en is mixed in 'mongs' de yuthers. I ain' skeered ter eat de grapes, 'caze I knows de old vimes fum de noo ones; but wid strangers dey ain' no tellin' w'at mought happen. I wouldn' 'vise yer ter buy dis vimya'd" (*Conjure*, 43).

Despite this reiterated advice, Julius has really said nothing to dissuade John from buying the vineyard, and he knows it. In fact, his precise numerical account of the grapevine's rich yields prior to Mars Dugal's original invocation of conjure to disrupt the plantation economy can only encourage John to expect a successful investment. Moreover, to suggest that Julius hopes to convince John of the danger of an antebellum spell, cast by an African-American conjure woman, is to underestimate Julius's shrewdness as a judge of character, for he knows that in John's "coolness of judgement" conjure is nothing but a pagan superstition (*Conjure*, 32). Why, then, does Julius tell Henry's story? If he doesn't intend to frighten John out of purchasing the plantation, what does he hope to gain, and how does his story serve his interests?

There is no simple answer to these questions, but something like an explanation might lie in Julius's closing image of the grapevine. After the Yankee's disastrous intervention, the old vines "did 'pear ter die," Julius explains, "but a few un 'em come out ag'in, en is mixed in 'mongs' de yuthers" (*Conjure*, 43). Having suffered through successive periods of "shiftless cultivation" and "utter neglect" since the war, the vines twine "themselves among the slender branches of the saplings which had sprung up among them," presenting a vivid image of horticultural—not to say cultural—blending and hybridization (*Conjure*, 32–33). "Grape culture is a trope for culture itself" in "The Goophered Grapevine," according to Eric Sundquist, who points out that Julius possesses a vested interest in this image of the New South as a luxuriant, uncultivated, racially and culturally diverse world of hybrid possibilities.[12] Julius's tale moves in many directions at once, but the danger he consistently returns to, and the danger Julius faces in the present, involves the misguided and ultimately destructive effort to profit through the disfranchisement of blacks from this cultural image. Julius does not oppose John's investment in the plantation; indeed, he is wily enough to know that he may profit handsomely from an infusion of capital into the local economy. But his stake in the local economy, like that of other postwar African Americans in the fictional Patesville, most of whom turn out to be Julius's relatives, is radically uncertain, and it is this uncertainty that his tale is meant to address.

John will buy the grapevine, if both John and Julius have their way, but who will get the grapes? Chesnutt implies through his master-trope of the hopelessly knotted and twined grapevine that the grapes must be shared between black and white, old and new Southerners, as they were prior to the white master's resort to conjure, and as they are at the moment of John's arrival at the plantation, in the immediate wake of Reconstruction. Mars Dugal', like the antebellum Southern culture he represents, erred fatally by attempting through conjure to exclude African Americans from the very idea of Southern culture—to exclude them, that is, from the grapevine. Julius's tale is finally more cautionary and instructive than forbidding. His account of Henry's life and death serves as a warning to John less about the dangers of owning a goophered grapevine than about the dangers of repeating an old mistake, that of bisecting the local culture—and of destroying its organizing symbol in the process—to gratify an unregulated appetite for profit.

Describing the "arresting mixture of folktale, fantasy, and satiric comedy" that characterizes "The Goophered Grapevine," William Andrews points out that Chesnutt deliberately resisted the impulse to sentimentalize Henry's story, presenting the slave protagonist's death as "less pitiful than curious and weird" (Andrews, 61). This important insight has led many readers to compare the emotional effect of conjure to that of the blues, which Ralph Ellison eloquently described as the transcendence of suffering "not by the consolation of philosophy, but by squeezing from it a near-tragic, near-comic lyricism."[13] Chesnutt's art of literary conjure operates in this lyrical register between comedy and tragedy, often explicitly juxtaposing the energies of minstrel burlesque against those of a formulaic sentimentalism. In *The Conjure Woman*'s second tale, Julius exhibits his command of a new key, exchanging the minstrel trap-

pings of "The Goophered Grapevine" for the unrelenting sentimentality of "Po' Sandy," a tale full of human suffering in which Chesnutt
explores another dimension of conjure's impressive emotional range.

"Po' Sandy"

The opening sentence of "Po' Sandy" resounds with John's definitive
reference to "my vineyard in central North Carolina," a construction
that intends to put to rest important questions raised in the previous
story about black access to and control of plantation resources (*Conjure*,
44). As "The Goophered Grapevine" has already made clear, however,
such lexical bullying is effective mainly at convincing the bully of his
own strength, and questions of ownership remain very much alive in the
figurative realm of Julius's antebellum stories. In the face of such self-
assured proprietorship on John's part, Julius resorts to a new strategy to
accomplish his artful brand of economic subversion in "Po' Sandy,"
appealing this time not to John's capitalist instincts for prudent investment but to Annie's "sympathetic turn of mind" (*Conjure*, 45).

Annie's "poor health" was offered in "The Goophered Grapevine" as
the couple's ostensible reason for abandoning the northern Midwest in
favor of the "more equable" climate of North Carolina, but it is apparent throughout that story that John is less interested in improving his
wife's frail health than in acquiring ownership of undervalued industries
in a region where "labor was cheap, and land could be bought for a mere
song" (*Conjure*, 31). John's habitual conflation of the couple's therapeutic and industrial designs masks a crucial rift in his imperfect patriarchal
authority over the new Southern plantation, a rift that comes obscurely
into view at the beginning of "Po' Sandy," when John begrudgingly
acknowledges his wife's "occult reason" for wishing to build a new
kitchen "apart from the dwelling house, after the usual Southern fash-
ion" (*Conjure*, 44–45). This bid for separation on Annie's part does not
amount to a cry of marital despair, for she is hardly cognizant enough of
the sources of her chronic melancholy to articulate such a protest; but
Julius invests Annie's occult reasoning with implied significance by
spinning a yarn in which her proposed new kitchen provides a final resting place for Tenie, a slave woman driven mad with grief over the loss of
her husband. The unsentimental Mars Marrabo, Tenie's master and—
like Mars Dugal'—another avatar of the postbellum capitalist patriarch,
"didn' shed no tears," according to Julius. "He thought Tenie wuz crazy

... en dey ain' much room in dis worl' fer crazy w'ite folks, let 'lone a crazy nigger" (*Conjure*, 53).

With this blunt assertion of Annie's own peril as a "crazy" white woman in the postwar plantation regime, Julius invites Annie's identification with Tenie's tragic experience and effectively exploits John's insensitivity to her distress. In fact, Annie's role as a potential coadjutor in Julius's subversive performance has already been noted by John, who, in the story's opening frame, remarks condescendingly on a perceived intellectual affinity between African Americans and liberal women of Annie's class. Attributing the "strained attention" with which Annie receives Julius's tales to a childlike feminine excess of sentimentalism, John explains that Annie "takes a deep interest in the stories of plantation life which she hears from the lips of the older colored people. Some of these stories are quaintly humorous; others wildly extravagant, revealing the Oriental cast of the negro's imagination; while others, poured freely into the sympathetic ear of a Northern-bred woman, disclose many a tragic incident of the darker side of slavery" (*Conjure*, 46). As her response to Tenie's tragedy will demonstrate, Annie's interest in Julius's tales stems not from an imagined affinity for the quaint, the extravagant, and the oriental, but from her felt identification with the suffering of Julius's antebellum characters, an imaginative linkage between white and black, pre- and postwar worlds, that again calls to mind Chesnutt's image of the socially inclusive grapevine.

John's acquisitiveness, here expressed in his desire to gather lumber for construction of the new kitchen by tearing down a small frame house on the plantation, again inspires Julius to narrate an instructive parable, this time regarding a tragic attempt in antebellum times to construct just such a facility. Julius describes the tribulations of a slave named Sandy, who is such an unusually diligent and productive worker that his easygoing master lends him constantly to needy relatives and friends, depriving Sandy of a stable home and family. Sandy's sense of dispossession becomes increasingly acute, until he exclaims in anguish, "it 'pears ter me I ain' got no home, ner no marster, ner no mistiss, ner no nuffin" (*Conjure*, 47). This expression of the slave's dismay over the insecurity of his servile status resonates with the popular representation of African Americans as loyal retainers, grateful for the master's protection and support, a representation common in literary periodicals like the *Atlantic Monthly*, where "Po' Sandy" first appeared in May 1888. In Chesnutt's ironic rewriting of the plantation tradition, however, the slave's pursuit of a more permanent and inflexible servitude yields little to celebrate. When Sandy invites his beloved wife Tenie, a conjure woman, to change him into a tree so that he can no longer be moved around at his master's whim, he finds himself even more thoroughly commodified as a plantation resource than before. In addition to achieving a measure of resistance to Mars Marrabo's authority, Sandy's transformation perfects his reification, leaving him vulnerable to new forms of exploitation, as when another slave cuts painfully into his bark for turpentine.

Tenie's plans to rescue Sandy from this latest degradation are interrupted when she is sent to care for the master's daughter-in-law on another plantation, and while she is away "Mars Marrabo tuk a notion fer ter buil' im a noo kitchen" (*Conjure*, 50). When Tenie returns to find Sandy reduced to a stump, "wid sap runnin' out'n it, en de limbs layin' scattered roun', she 'nigh 'bout went out'n her min' " (*Conjure*, 50). Taken for a crazy woman when she appears at the sawmill, sobbing hysterically and holding a goopher antidote in her hands, Tenie is fastened to a post and forced to witness Sandy's destruction by the giant saw. Mars Marrabo builds his new kitchen, but it "wuzn' much use, fer it hadn' be'n put up long befo' de niggers 'mence' ter notice quare things erbout it. Dey could hear sump'n moanin' en groanin' 'bout de kitchen in de night-time ... lack it wuz in great pain en sufferin' " (*Conjure*, 52). The kitchen is soon torn down when Mars Marrabo's wife herself becomes terrified by the haunted lumber, which is later used to build a schoolhouse. There, weeks later, one of the children discovers Tenie, "layin' on de flo', still, en col', en dead," having grieved herself to death (*Conjure*, 52).

Julius concludes the tale by advising John against recycling the boards from the old schoolhouse, for "dat lumber ... is gwine ter be ha'nted tel de las' piece er plank is rotted en crumble' inter dus' " (*Conjure*, 53). As it later turns out, this advice is predictably informed by Julius's own plans for the property. Punning somewhat less subtly than usual, Chesnutt has Annie explain to her husband that "there has been a split in the Sandy Run Colored Baptist Church, on the temperance question," and that Julius has requested to use the building temporarily as a meetinghouse for the seceders.[14] " 'I hope you didn't let the old rascal have it,' " returns John, "with some warmth" (*Conjure*, 54). Annie admits that she has handed over the property, along with a contribution to the fledgling sect.

This cozy arrangement conveys a reassuring impression of John's mastery of the situation, though it should be remembered that neither mastery nor degradation is ever total in Chesnutt's world of conjure. John condones Julius's petty maneuvering for control of the schoolhouse, and he apparently even derives some amusement from such limited expressions of resistance to his authority, amusement for which he is willing to pay in favors of the sort Julius earns here. As a fellow entrepreneur, John appreciates the economic self-interest that ostensibly motivates Julius's storytelling, and he interprets the stories in terms of that motivation. But to understand Julius's tales as mere utilitarian instruments meant to preserve token economic privileges is to understand them as John does, which is to say partially and superficially. The conjure stories *are*, as John appreciates, a form of postwar currency with which Julius bargains for specific material goods, but the stories also resonate with meanings that John's model of interpretation significantly cannot accommodate.

Thus while he is fully prepared for Julius's self-interested advice regarding the construction of the new kitchen—and fully prepared to reject that advice with condescending "warmth" of feeling—John is unprepared for Annie's reaction to the story, which introduces other possibilities for interpretation: " 'What a system it was,' she exclaimed, when Julius had finished, 'under which such things were possible!' " (*Conjure*, 53). John is understandably stunned by his wife's apparent profession of belief in Julius's account of human transformation. "What things?" he asks in amazement. "Are you seriously considering the possibility of a man's being turned into a tree?" Annie responds, "Oh, no ... not that"; and then, as if to imply that she has heard a very different story than the one John so casually dismisses as a product of Julius's scheming imagination, Annie mumbles absently, "poor Tenie!" (*Conjure*, 53).

The couple's inconsistent reactions again mark the rift between their differing sensibilities, and Julius has designed his tale for the very purpose of exploiting this rift.[15] As John's reaction to Annie indicates, he has listened to an exotic fairy tale of antebellum times, intended to influence his utilization of plantation resources in the present. Annie, on the other hand, has heard a tale that might have been entitled "Po' Tenie" rather than "Po' Sandy," a moving and perfectly believable account of one woman's psychological unraveling as a result of her isolation within the patriarchal regime of the old plantation. Julius's forcing comparison at the end of the tale—"dey ain' much room in dis' worl' fer crazy w'ite folks, let 'lone a crazy nigger"—serves to intimidate Annie, not with the prospect of a haunted kitchen, as John assumes, but with the specter of her own superfluous status on the plantation. The story is like a wake-up call for Annie in that it allegorizes her melancholy and recommends a crucial disruption in the cultural conditions that produce it. "That night," John explains, "after we had gone to bed, and my wife had to all appearances been sound asleep for half an hour, she startled me out of an incipient doze by exclaiming suddenly,— 'John, I don't believe I want my new kitchen built out of the lumber in that old schoolhouse' " (*Conjure*, 53).

While John can understand this reversal only as evidence of his wife's intellectual susceptibility to the most absurd fantasies, Annie's rejection of the haunted lumber is really an expression of resistance. Having derived therapeutic value from Julius's yarn, she declines to pursue Tenie's fate, the fate of the female melancholic. Moreover, in asking John to build the kitchen exclusively with new lumber, Annie implicitly refuses to perpetuate the dehumanizing economics of slavery into the postwar era. Through her influence, Julius acquires not only a meeting-house, but, much more significantly, a measure of control over the plantation past, which has a way of insinuating itself into the present of *The Conjure Woman* in the form of economic relations that persist in disfranchising African Americans. "Po' Sandy" might thus be taken as an exemplary tale for its illustration of at least one complex function of conjure, which here serves paradoxically to evoke the antebellum past as a strategy for keeping the past at bay.

"Mars Jeems's Nightmare"

Annie's insistence on using new lumber for her kitchen, instead of Sandy's mutilated remains, amounts to a subtle intervention into what was, in 1888, the increasingly threatening historical continuity of pre- and postwar Southern race relations; yet it is a symbolic intervention, and one that John has no trouble ignoring. In fact, Julius's veiled resistance to John's new Southern hegemony—which often dangerously resembles the old Southern hegemony of figures like Mars Dugal' and Mars McAdoo—typically does more to reinforce than to dislodge John's racist assumptions about African-American character and personality.[16] Thus after the sentimental tour de force of "Po' Sandy," with its understated rejection of John's authority to extend the degradation of Sandy and Tenie into the postwar era, John introduces *The Conjure Woman*'s next story with a self-assured analysis of the lingering effects of slavery on Julius's imagination.

He was a marvelous hand in the management of horses and dogs, with whose mental processes he manifested a greater familiarity than mere use would seem to account for, though it was doubtless due to the simplicity of a life that had kept him close to nature. Toward my tract of land and the things that were on it ... he maintained a peculiar personal attitude, what might be called predial rather than proprietary. He had been accustomed, until long after middle life, to look upon himself as the property of another. When this relation was no longer possible, owing to the war, and to his master's death and the dispersion of the family, he had been unable to break off entirely the mental habits of a lifetime, but had attached himself to the old plantation, of which he seemed to consider himself an appurtenance. (*Conjure*, 55)

Julius assiduously cultivates this image of himself as the victim of "mental habits" that persist in limiting the freedman's realization of his full humanity, even as his parables of plantation life tell a very different story about the causes and effects of the sort of reification John here attributes to the ex-slave's inescapable psychological predicament. The stories themselves, with their nuanced resistance to John's proprietary zeal, betray levels of self-consciousness in Julius that John's theory of the black "appurtenance" cannot encompass, yet it suits Julius's purposes to foster John's impression of the ex-slave's affinity with the "mental processes" of horses and dogs. By maintaining the pretense of a "predial rather than proprietary" relation to John's land "and the things that were on it," Julius asserts his claim to the property in terms that are flattering to John. But what of Julius's progeny? How can his claim, masked as it is in self-effacing stereotype, be passed on to a generation of African Americans who never experienced slavery and who are therefore unfit to put on Julius's obsequious disguise? This is the complicated sociological issue raised in "Mars Jeems's Nightmare," in which John's lengthy ruminations on the sources of Julius's "peculiar personal attitude" toward the plantation contrast sharply with his indignation toward another "type" of African-American character.[17]

At the beginning of the story, Julius solicits employment for his grandson, Tom, "a colored boy of about seventeen," whom John hires to do odd jobs around the house (*Conjure*, 55). But John's unfavorable first impressions are soon confirmed when Tom proves to be "very trifling" (*Conjure*, 56). Lacking the servile instincts ostensibly preserved in ex-slaves like Julius, Tom impresses his new employer with his "laziness, his carelessness, and his apparent lack of any sense of responsibility," marking him in John's view as a representative postwar African

American—or "new negro," in the contemporary phraseology—devoid of those predial "mental habits" cultivated under the old order (*Conjure,* 56).[18] The challenge for Julius in this story, then, is not to assert his right to the use of plantation resources, as in both "The Goophered Grapevine" and "Po' Sandy"—that right is granted, albeit at a price, in John's paternalistic opening remarks. Rather, Julius is concerned here about securing a viable economic role on the plantation for subsequent generations of his family, African Americans who have outgrown the minstrel mask and who must therefore encounter John's racism squarely.[19]

Julius seizes an opportunity to deliver another of his ambiguously instructive yarns while Annie and John recline in their "rockaway" coach, waiting for a man to finish the symbolic task of clarifying the local mineral spring from which they intend to gather water "for sanitary reasons." John explains that "[i]t was often necessary to wait awhile in North Carolina; and our Northern energy had not been entirely proof against the influences of climate and local custom," a comment that recalls the "native infection of restfulness" that besets the couple in "The Goophered Grapevine" (*Conjure,* 57, 33). John's medical analogy ironically associates Northern energy with health and Southern restfulness with disease, despite indications of Annie's gradual recovery under the potent "influences of climate and local custom." Foremost among these infectious influences, of course, are Julius's narrative performances, which typically encourage a "clarifying of the moral faculty" comparable to the cleansing of the spring that proceeds while John and Annie listen to the tale of old Mars Jeems McLean.[20]

Julius's story is occasioned by the sight of "young Mistah McLean," grandson of the antebellum patriarch, who beats his horse furiously as he rides past the stalled rockaway, inspiring Julius to draw an ominous connection: "A man w'at 'buses his hoss is gwine ter be ha'd on de folks w'at wuks fer 'im" (*Conjure,* 57). Old Mars Jeems was such a man, "monst'us stric' wid his han's" and unwilling to make allowances for what Julius describes as the "nachul bawn laz'ness" of his slaves (*Conjure,* 58). Jeems drives them so ruthlessly that his fiancée breaks off their engagement out of fear that "he mought git so useter 'busin' his niggers dat he'd 'mence ter 'buse his wife atter he got useter habbin' her roun' de house" (*Conjure,* 58). The chain of brutalization leading from the white man's horse, to his servants, to his wife is designed to enlist Annie's sympathy for the plight of Julius's slave protagonist, Solomon, who appeals to Aunt Peggy's powers of conjure to modify Mars Jeems's excessive discipline. Peggy notes that she "has ter be kinder keerful 'bout cunj'in' w'ite folks," but she agrees to prepare a goopher mixture that will transform Jeems into a black man, thus exposing him to the effects of his own cruelty (*Conjure*, 60).

When the "noo nigger" arrives at the plantation the following day as payment for a debt, his confusion and disorientation are immediately interpreted by the overseer, Nick Johnson, as "laziness en impidence," for which he receives a violent whipping. Repeated whippings fail to make a docile slave out of the rebellious newcomer, whom Mr. Johnson finally returns to the neighbor who brought him rather than bear the risk of destroying a valuable commodity. After the "noo nigger" 's departure, Jeems suddenly reappears on the plantation, bruised and ragged, complaining to Solomon of a "monst'us bad dream,—fac', a reg'lar, nach'ul nightmare" (*Conjure*, 65). Winding up his story, Julius explains that upon his return, Jeems became "a noo man," expressing his humanity by firing the overseer and relaxing the strict discipline of the plantation. In return for his leniency, Jeems experiences a simultaneous increase in his slave population and in his cotton crop, and when his former fiancée hears about "de noo gwines-on" on Mars Jeems's plantation, she takes him back, "en 'fo' long dey had a fine weddin', en all de darkies had a big feas', en dey wuz fiddlin' en dancin' en funnin' en frolic'in' fum sundown 'tel mawnin' " (*Conjure*, 68).

Mars Jeems's transformation is one of those events in Chesnutt's fiction that invites a problematic series of interpretations. On one hand, the story seems to provide a virulently racist apology for the enslavement of African Americans, in that Jeems—the white man in black skin—proves to be inherently masterful in defiance of tyranny, unlike his meek fellow slaves, who cower under Mr. Johnson's whip. Julius even speculates that the "noo nigger" might have "made it wa'm fer Ole Nick," "ef some er de yuther niggers hadn' stop' 'im" (*Conjure*, 62). With its harmonious closing image of the restored master/slave relationship, the story would seem to endorse widely accepted assumptions about African-American docility and fitness for service, in contrast to the aggressive tendencies of the "Angry-Saxon race," as a black character in *The Marrow of Tradition* describes his revered superiors.[21] Moreover, in summarizing the moral of Jeems's ordeal, Julius seems intent upon making this reading of the tale available by reminding John of the benefits enjoyed by "w'ite folks" who make " 'lowance fer po' ign'ant niggers" (*Conjure*, 68). Preaching leniency for an inferior race whose main characteristic is "nachul bawn laz'ness," Julius appears to gratify John's sense of racial mastery to achieve petty financial gains in the form of continued employment for his "trifling" grandson.

Yet this interpretation of the story is dangled in front of John like a carrot in front of a mule. Mars Jeems's transformation into a "noo nigger" does offer to gratify white racist assumptions, but the story also provides a remarkably subtle commentary on Tom's uncertain predicament as a "new negro" in the postwar plantation setting. Born in freedom and thus unfit to assume the servile role in which he is cast by Aunt Peggy's conjure, Jeems becomes the story's instructive representative of Tom's dilemma. Upon his arrival at the plantation as a black man, Jeems is immediately thrust into an inflexible and perfectly unfamiliar identity when Mr. Johnson addresses him as "Sambo." While he rejects this designation (" 'My name ain' Sambo,' 'spon' de noo nigger"), he cannot explain with certainty who he is, or where he comes from ("My head is kin' er mix' up"), and so receives a beating for his apparent obstinacy (*Conjure*, 61–62). But Jeems, like Tom, is far less obstinate than simply ignorant about how to inhabit a stereotype he has known heretofore only from the outside. His "laziness en impidence"— which explicitly recall Tom's "laziness," "carelessness," and "lack of responsibility"—are the products of his unfitness for the servile role in which he has been cast, an unfitness based not on racial characteristics fixed in nature but on inadequate training in the Sambo act. Thus when he is put to work, Jeems "didn' 'pear ter know how ter han'le a hoe," and again his failure is interpreted as willful resistance (*Conjure*, 62). Like Tom, who is unable or unwilling to gratify John with traditional tokens of deference and respect, the "noo nigger" just couldn't " 'pear ter git it th'oo his min' dat he was a slabe en had ter wuk en min' de w'ite folks" (*Conjure*, 62).

Members of the "noo" generation, Julius's grandchildren, will never get this idea entirely through their heads, the story implies, and while they may not yet have developed a coherent response to Mr. Johnson's circular query—"W'at's yo' name, Sambo?"—they no longer wear the Sambo stereotype like a disguise. In a passage that bears some relevance to "Mars Jeems's Nightmare," General Belmont, a character in *The Marrow of Tradition*, compliments his friend Major Carteret by noting that the Major's servant, Jerry, is "not one of your new negroes, who think themselves as good as white men, and want to run the government. Jerry knows his place,—he is respectful, humble, obedient, and content with the face and place assigned to him by nature" (*Marrow*, 281). While Chesnutt's fiction constantly works to revise this pejorative characterization of postwar African Americans, he would concur with the General in identifying Tom as "one of your new negroes," a man who has literally forgotten his place in the culture of the plantation. Tom's shortcomings as a servant, Julius implies, have less to do with inherent laziness than with the effects of a major cultural transformation in African-American life, a transformation as disorienting as Mars Jeems's nightmare.

If the "noo nigger" can be taken as a figure for the "new negro" of the postwar era, Jeems's transformation back into a white man at the end of the story suggests yet another compelling irony. Julius comments that after his ordeal, "a change come ober Mars Jeems," for Aunt Peggy's goopher had "made a noo man un 'im enti'ely" (*Conjure*, 67). This "noo man," like the "noo nigger," is a postwar revision of an antebellum type, a white Southern patriarch attuned to the social and political changes wrought by war and emancipation—a figure associated inevitably with John himself, just as Jeems in the role of the "noo nigger" invites comparison with Tom.

But whereas Julius has taken pains to show that the "new negro" cannot be expected to assume the role of the old, his story ends by saying something very different about the social and political transformation of whites. Describing the change that comes over Mars Jeems after his restoration, Julius notes that "he tol' de han's dey neenter wuk on'y fum sun ter sun, en he cut dey tasks down so dey didn' nobody had ter stan' ober 'em wid a rawhide er a hick'ry" (*Conjure*, 67–68). This is noticeably a change in the degree of violence exercised against blacks, rather than a change in the master's kind of authority, and herein lies the story's shrewdest comment on the inequities of the postwar era. As the plantation's new patriarch, John is certainly more benevolent and progressive than his antebellum counterpart, but the change may be one of degree rather than of kind, betraying the evolution of the antebellum slaveholder into "a noo man ... enti'ely" as something of a cultural fiction. When he learns that Annie has rehired Tom despite his firm decision, John adopts the reactionary tone of General Belmont on the subject of "new negroes," declaring: "I did not share my wife's rose-colored hopes in regard to Tom; but as I did not wish the servants to think there was any conflict of authority in the household, I let the boy stay" (*Conjure*, 69). The large-scale social changes symbolized by Jeems's transformation into a "noo nigger" have produced a new set of conditions for African-American identity, Chesnutt suggests, conditions that the "noo" white man struggles somewhat pathetically to ignore.

"The Conjurer's Revenge"

Julius's next tale of symbolic metamorphosis, "The Conjurer's Revenge," offers another veiled critique of slavery and its postwar legacy, though with the important difference that conjure here operates exclusively within a black male world.[22] There is no exploitative white master in this story, and conjure serves not as an instrument of resistance to oppression but as one black man's technique for exacting cruel revenge upon another. Responding to this fundamental shift in direction, Annie objects when the tale is over: "That story does not appeal to me, Uncle Julius, and is not up to your usual mark. It isn't pathetic, it has no moral that I can discover, and I can't see why you should tell it. In fact, it seems to me like nonsense" (*Conjure*, 79). Annie's disapproval is partly justified, for affirmation of the slave's humanity seems to be conspicuously absent from this tale about the transformation of a man into a mule. Conjure is a purely malevolent force in "The Conjurer's Revenge," rather than a last resort for discouraged slave lovers and families as in "Po' Sandy" and "Mars Jeems's Nightmare," and Julius's story offers no trap door through which to invite Annie's identification with the tragedy of Primus's degradation.[23] Yet the man-mule's unavailability to human sympathy, black or white, while it grates on Annie's sensibilities, is itself an important aspect of Julius's tale, which allegorizes both the condition of slavery generally and the special case of "mulatto" identity.

The story opens with a portrait of boredom verging on melancholy, as John catalogs the Northern couple's bourgeois entertainments—newspapers, magazines, a "fairly good library," a "passable baritone" voice—and testifies to their ineffectiveness at breaking "the monotony of Sabbath quiet" (*Conjure*, 70, 72). In this enervating cultural milieu, Annie ploughs "conscientiously" through a missionary report, while John seeks diversion in "the impossible career of the blonde heroine of a rudimentary novel." To rescue the couple from their literary doldrums, Julius appears before the piazza, advancing "with a dignity of movement quite different from his week-day slouch" (*Conjure*, 70). His Sabbath "dignity" is a puzzling touch, for, as Annie realizes, Julius's story trades on the couple's desire for entertainment in the most undignified way. John initiates the performance by asking for advice about the development of some new land, to which Julius responds that the horses have all they can do already. When John agrees that a new mule will be necessary, Julius objects with a shake of his head, finally explaining: "Fac' is ... I doan lack ter dribe a mule. I's alluz afeared I mought be imposin' on some human creetur; eve'y time I cuts a mule wid a hick'ry, 'pears ter me mos' lackly I's cuttin' some er my own relations, er somebody e'se w'at can't he'p deyse'ves" (*Conjure*, 71).

Julius's assertion of kinship with mules plays on the etymological origin of the word "mulatto," insinuating a hereditary parallel between two presumably degenerate and unnatural species. According to John in "The Goophered Grapevine," Julius himself possesses "a slight strain of other than negro blood," so that his premise in this story conveys a strikingly negative personal representation, in contrast to the "dignity of movement" with which he appears to John in the opening frame (*Conjure*, 34). Responding to Julius's apparent willingness to occupy a demeaning stereotype for the sake of her entertainment, Annie objects again to Julius's indulgence in such "ridiculous nonsense," but the impending story not surprisingly possesses interest for John, who employs "diplomacy" to urge the storyteller on (*Conjure*, 72).

Julius's protagonist in this tale is a "club-footed nigger" named Primus, at one time the liveliest hand on Mars Jim McGee's plantation, "alluz a-dancin', en drinkin', en runnin' roun', en singin', en pickin' de banjo; 'cep'n once in a w'ile, w'en he'd git so sulky en stubborn dat de w'ite folks couldn' ha'dly do nuffin wid 'im" (*Conjure*, 72). Primus's stubbornness and high spirits, mulelike qualities that will later smooth his transformation into a new physical state, establish him in a unique liminal status on the plantation. Unlike other slaves, he enjoys freedom of movement and is exempt from the master's discipline: "Primus didn' min' de rules, en went w'en he felt like it; en de w'ite folks purten' lack dey didn' know it, fer Primus was dange'ous w'en he got in dem stubborn spells, en dey'd ruther not fool wid 'im" (*Conjure*, 72). In his special status Primus consorts with the "free niggers" down on "de Wim'l'-ton Road," dancing until two in the morning and returning to the quarters with impunity. While he enjoys unheard-of privileges for a slave, however, Primus is not free, and his predicament introduces its own set of difficulties, suggestive for Chesnutt of the problematic conditions of mixed-race identity. Those difficulties arise significantly not through the agency of an overbearing white master, but as the result of vindictive measures taken by a conjure man of recent African descent, who avenges Primus's theft of a shoat by complicating his already uncertain racial identity. As punishment for his theft, Primus is turned into a mule—or, by association, a "mulatto"—a "human creetur" who enjoys certain privileges at the expense of his identification with either the slave or the free community, neither of which any longer acknowledges him as a member.

His new role appears to suit Primus about as well as the old one, except that his problematic social status has become even more pronounced. As a mule, he still enjoys freedoms that exceed anything allowed to slaves, as when he gorges himself on tobacco or drinks a barrel of wine. Instead of punishment for these serious infractions of plantation discipline, Primus is merely left alone to sleep off his hangover, just as he used to escape disciplinary consequences prior to his transformation. But these freedoms come at a price, for Primus as mule, like Primus as man, lives outside any human community, and his exemption from white discipline entails exclusion from black social life. Accordingly, his wife takes up with a man named Dan, and Primus is reduced to peering in from the cabin window, "wid his lips drawed back over his toofs, grinnin' en snappin' at Dan des' lack he wanter eat 'im up" (*Conjure*, 76). This comical image of the man-mule pitifully suspended between irreconcilable states of freedom and bondage, socially isolated from the story's white and black communities, resonates with Chesnutt's frequent journal observations about his own untenable status as a mixed-race Southerner, who is "neither 'nigger,' poor white, nor 'buckrah' ... [t]oo stuck up for the colored folks, and, of course, not recognized by the whites" (*Journals*, 157–58). Primus's transformation into a mule, Chesnutt suggests, only consolidates his isolation as a figure trapped between two worlds, like the young nurse in *The Marrow of Tradition*, who occupies "the border line between two irreconcilable states of life," possessing "neither the picturesqueness of the slave, nor the unconscious dignity of those for whom freedom has been the immemorial birthright" (*Marrow*, 245).

As the analogy between these two similarly situated characters implies, the significance of Primus's dilemma extends beyond the conditions of mixed-race identity to encompass the historical predicament of African Americans generally after the war. This broadening of the story's frame of reference becomes clear toward the end, when the suddenly Christianized and repentant conjure man attempts to apply a goopher antidote that will restore Primus to his original condition. Before he can complete the process, however, the conjure man dies, and Primus is left on suggestively unsure footing, literally straddling two worlds with his two feet, one animal and the other human. As a parable about black life in the American South, then, the story describes Primus's incomplete recovery of manhood in the postwar aftermath of his dehumanizing experience as a beast of burden under the rule of slavery. Perhaps more subtly, however, the story anticipates Chesnutt's non-dialect fiction by underscoring the crippling effect of the "mulatto" designation in a culture that conceives of black and white identities according to its blind faith in the integrity of the color line.

Annie's failure to understand why Julius should tell such a morbid tale is instructive here. Unlike John, she recognizes the economic pretext for Julius's performance (he expects to earn a commission on John's purchase of a horse rather than a mule) as incidental to the meaning of the story, which seems to hinge on Julius's demeaning characterization of Primus and himself as blood relatives to the mule family. Julius responds to her skepticism with a significant reproach:

> Dey's so many things a body knows is lies, dat dey ain' no use gwine roun' findin' fault wid tales dat mought des ez well be so ez not. F' instance, dey's a young nigger gwine ter school in town, en he come out heah de yuther day en 'lowed dat de sun stood still en de yeath turnt roun' eve'y day on a kinder axletree. (*Conjure*, 79)

Julius dismisses this Copernican abstraction by insisting on the truth of appearances: "ef a man can't b'lieve w'at 'e sees, I can't see no use in libbin'." His comment is designed at one level to manipulate John, who will exclaim at the end of the story, "Alas for the deceitfulness of appearances!" after he has foolishly purchased a broken-down horse from Julius's friend. But Julius's epistemological preference for appearances over abstractions, self-serving though it may be, might also be understood as a critique of the sort of abstract racial logic that stigmatizes and isolates the mixed-race American. "[E]f a man can't b'lieve w'at 'e sees ... ," Julius continues, "mought 's well die en be whar we can't see nuffin." What one sees in Chesnutt's fictional Patesville, like what Chesnutt saw throughout his youth in the actual Fayetteville, is abundant evidence of physical and cultural "admixture," "the imperfect blending of old with new, of race with race, of slavery with freedom" (*Marrow*, 245). Primus's suffering is perhaps neither as pointless nor as demeaning to Julius as Annie assumes, for while the story significantly fails to generate her identification with the protagonist's anguished condition, Julius quietly critiques a culture that refuses to believe in what it sees, a culture that defines the "mulatto" as a racial abstraction and makes him invisible by burying his identity in a bestial metaphor. Enthralled by race consciousness in its manifold antebellum and postbellum forms, white and black Patesvillians deny that Primus represents the cultural norm, a norm expressed most succinctly in Chesnutt's image of the chaotically intertwined postbellum grapevine. So Primus remains trapped between seemingly irreconcilable cultural options, neither free nor slave, neither man nor mule, a victim not of the "mulatto"'s presumed affinity with the mule, but of his culture's refusal to acknowledge his complete humanity.

This reading of the story as a critique of racial abstractions that persist in dehumanizing African Americans long after the war tends to obscure an important question about Julius's role in *The Conjure Woman* generally. The question might be put simply as follows: in narrating the story of a black man's fluid transformation into a mule, doesn't Julius purchase symbolic resistance (and a new suit) at a terrific price, in that his tale perpetuates a racist stereotype? Primus at the end of "The Conjurer's Revenge" is literally a "human creetur," living confirmation of John's outrageously condescending view in "Mars Jeems's Nightmare" that African Americans are the intellectual cousins of horses and dogs. As Ben Slote has pointed out, the conjure stories tread perilously close to this sort of backhanded endorsement of racist assumptions, in that Julius's tales always threaten to gratify the same racial iconography they subvert (Slote 689–90). This delicate rhetorical balance has sometimes been taken as a measure of *The Conjure Woman*'s ineffectiveness as social criticism, and Chesnutt himself bridled under the limitations imposed on his art by Julius's ambivalent relation to the plantation past.

Yet Chesnutt's most compelling ironies respond directly to such rhetorical limitations. A case in point is the closing image of Julius in "The Conjurer's Revenge," dressed in a new Sunday suit that recalls his dignified appearance in Sabbath array at the beginning of the story. As the repetition of this image implies, Julius's narrative performance—his demeaning and, to Annie, offensive assertion of "mulatto" kinship with mules—bears explicit relation to his "dignity of movement" at the beginning and end of the story. The suit, in other words, is Julius's token for a much more significant commodity, and its appearance in the closing image allows Chesnutt to frame the crucial question at the heart of all the conjure tales: can dignity be purchased with humiliation? The dialect stories are far better at asking than at answering this question, though Chesnutt's persistent desire to leave the plantation formula behind implies that the sort of compromises that produced his subtlest ironies were, for him, finally too costly.

"Sis' Becky's Pickaninny"

The "Sabbath quiet" that hangs over John's plantation like a dark cloud in "The Conjurer's Revenge" has become a monotonous silence in "Sis' Becky's Pickaninny," Julius's next conjure story, and Annie consequently falls victim to a "settled melancholy, attended with vague forebodings of impending misfortune" (*Conjure*, 82).[24] On the advice of her physician, who ambiguously warns that "[t]his melancholy lowers her tone too much," John employs a variety of "expedients" intended to raise Annie's spirits:

> I read novels to her. I had the hands on the place come up in the evening and serenade her with plantation songs. Friends came in some- times and talked, and frequent letters from the North kept her in touch with her former home. But nothing seemed to rouse her from the depression into which she had fallen. (*Conjure*, 82)

When Julius appears with a rabbit's foot in his hand and a story on his lips, John speculates that one of the old man's plantation tales "might interest my wife as much or more than the novel I had meant to read from" (*Conjure*, 84). His intuition proves correct, but not for the reasons that lead John to group Julius's performance with his own ineffective therapeutic expedients. Instead of another culturally sanctioned form of diversion, the story of Sis' Becky picks up where "Po' Sandy" left off, developing a pointed critique of John's rational understanding of Annie's illness.

Julius's folk diagnosis and remedy for Annie's chronic depression hinge on faith in the talismanic power of "de lef' hin'-foot er a grabe- ya'd rabbit, killt by a cross-eyed nigger on a da'k night in de full er de moon" (*Conjure*, 83). When Julius admits that he carries the rabbit's foot for luck, John seizes the opportunity to deliver a lecture on the vagaries of African-American folk belief: " 'Julius,' I observed, half to him and half to my wife, 'your people will never rise in the world until they throw off these childish superstitions and learn to live by the light of reason and common sense' " (*Conjure*, 83). The arrogant rationalism of this speech is directed "half to my wife" because Annie has already betrayed a dangerous susceptibility to "influences of climate and local custom" (*Conjure*, 57). Indeed, John's importation of literature and cor- respondence from the North intends to counteract the "native infection of restfulness" that he suspects may be responsible for her worsening condition (*Conjure*, 33).[25] Always critical of Annie's feminine sympathy for what he calls in "Po' Sandy" "the Oriental cast of the negro's imagination," John here offers a joint diagnosis of her emotional illness and of Julius's arrested cultural and intellectual development, attributing both to an unhealthy neglect of "reason and common sense" (*Conjure*, 46).

Apparently unimpressed by this effort to bully him out of a traditional belief, Julius offers the story of Sis' Becky as ostensible proof of the charm's power to bring good luck. Taking his cue from Harriet Beecher Stowe, Frances E. W. Harper, and other sentimental storytellers of the period, he constructs the tale around the powerful emotional bond between Becky and her baby boy, Mose, "de cutes', blackes', shiny-eyedes' little nigger you ebber laid eyes on" (*Conjure*, 84). Becky's master, Kunnel Pen'leton, is a "kin'-hea'ted man" who does not believe in breaking up slave families as a rule, but whose benevolent instincts are obscured by an aristocratic weakness for fine horses. Thus he exchanges Becky for a champion racehorse, after which both she and Mose sink into a chronic depression that bears striking resemblance to Annie's "settled melancholy." To ward off the "impending misfortune" apparently in store for both mother and child, Mose's guardian appeals to Aunt Peggy, who arranges for occasional visitations by transforming Mose into a bird. When his flights to Becky's distant plantation become too much of a burden, Aunt Peggy instructs a hornet to sting Kunnel Pen'leton's new horse in the knees so that he will appear lame, and at the same time casts a goopher spell over Becky, who retires to bed in anticipation of her own imminent death. Becky's new master laughs at her foolish belief in witchcraft, "fer he wuz one er dese yer w'ite folks w'at purten' dey doan b'liebe in conj'in," but he cannot convince Becky that her illness is imaginary (*Conjure*, 91). The two white men finally agree to call off the trade, each one convinced he has acquired a worthless property, and Becky is allowed to return to Mose, who showers her with love and later cares for her in old age.

John responds to this sentimental conclusion with sarcasm, complimenting Julius on having devised "a very ingenious fairy tale," but Annie objects "severely" to his pejorative tone. "Why, John!" she exclaims, "the story bears the stamp of truth, if ever a story did" (*Conjure*, 92). John notes that Annie "listened to this story with greater interest than she had manifested in any subject for several days," and he marvels at the "delightful animation" with which she defends its veracity (*Conjure*, 92). Although pleased by her sudden recovery of spirit, John cannot resist the opportunity to poke fun at Julius by pointing out that the story has decisively failed as a logical demonstration of the power of the rabbit's foot. Julius invites Annie, who possesses a sensitive ear for the logic and meaning of his stories, to explain the point:

> "I rather suspect," replied my wife promptly, "that Sis' Becky had no rabbit's foot."
> "You is hit de bull's-eye de fus' fire, ma'm," assented Julius. "Ef Sis' Becky had had a rabbit's foot, she nebber would 'a' went th'oo all dis trouble." (*Conjure*, 92)

Of course, this dubious conclusion proves only that Julius adheres to very different standards of veracity than John, for whom "the stamp of truth" is a poor substitute for rational certainty. Indeed, Julius's account of Sis' Becky's misfortune does not even pretend to verify his belief in the power of the rabbit's foot, for to do so would be to meet John on his own rational terms, terms that are inherently unsympathetic to African-American folk belief. Instead of proof, Julius offers an allusive critique of the moral implications of skepticism by equating John's position with the horse trader's self-serving disbelief in conjure. To dismiss conjure as a form of superstition, Julius implies, is to question the reality of Becky's acute suffering over the loss of her child. Thus while the trader rationalizes his cruel separation of mother and son by attributing Becky's illness to fantasy, conjure operates as a force of resistance—perhaps psychological, perhaps not—to the dehumanizing logic whereby horses are exchanged for human beings. Faith in its power to influence such transactions amounts to belief in the irreducibility of human beings into commodities. John's opinion that African Americans—and white Northern women—would be better off without such "childish superstitions" is thus freighted with problematic significance, for while Julius does not prove the validity of folk traditions to John's satisfaction, he does very effectively associate John's skepticism with the trader's questionable therapeutic disposition. Becky's master, according to Julius, "lafft at her, en argyed wid her, en tried ter 'suade her out'n dis yer fool notion, ez he called it ... but hit wa'n't no use. Sis' Becky kep' gettin' wusser en wusser, 'tel fin'lly dis yer man 'lowed Sis' Becky wuz gwine ter die, sho' nuff" (*Conjure*, 91).

John does not laugh at Annie, but his condescension toward Julius's folk beliefs is directed at least half in her direction, implying that John's disbelief in the legitimacy of the rabbit's foot as a cure may be taken as an extension of his disbelief in the reality of the illness itself. Moreover, if John's insensitivity can be linked to the horse trader's treatment of Becky, Annie clearly responds to the promise of the rabbit's foot for the same reasons that Becky stubbornly maintains her confidence in the power of Aunt Peggy's conjure. In the story's opening frame, John speculates that Julius's charm "must be very rare and valuable," to which Julius replies significantly: "dey ain' no 'mount er money could buy mine, suh" (*Conjure*, 83). This might appear like hyperbole, and Julius has surely proven himself a willing salesman in other tales, but here he asserts a crucial distinction between the intrinsic value of a sacred object—an object of faith—and the negotiable value of commodities exchanged in a cash economy dominated by men like Kunnel Pen'leton and the horse trader, white men of the sort that "purten' dey doan b'liebe in conj'in'."[26] The horse trader's rational disbelief, like John's skepticism, is a demystifying gesture, which amounts to the proposition that everything, including a rabbit's foot, has a price. "Childish superstitions" emerge here as the basis for a humanitarian vision which asserts that *not* everything is for sale, that some things—including the bond between mother and child—possess intrinsic value that cannot be reduced to a cash equivalent. This is the "truth" that Annie responds to with "delightful animation" at the end of the story, for Julius has effectively invited her identification with Becky as a victim of the reckless drift of abstract rationality, offering the rabbit's foot as a latter-day expression of the same belief system that protects Becky from the final humiliation of separation from Mose. In response to John's sermon on the culturally neutral virtues of reason and common sense, Julius indirectly asserts that such protection is still needed in the postwar era.

To John, the tale of Sis' Becky has arrived at the tautological conclusion that faith in the power of the rabbit's foot exists for those who already believe in the power of the rabbit's foot, but this circular reasoning only enhances the didactic effect of the tale for the listener Julius cares about most. No amount of money could convince Julius to sell his charm, but he asserts his willingness to "len' it ter anybody I sot sto' by" (*Conjure*, 83). Recognizing Annie as a victim of forces he understands all too well, forces to which she possesses no traditional cultural response, Julius offers a therapy suited to her illness. Numerous critics have speculated on the sexual implications of Julius's clandestine insertion of the rabbit's foot into the hidden pocket of Annie's dress, and indeed John does appear to have been symbolically "cuckolded and emasculated by Julius" as a result of their complicated exchange of ideas.[27] But the sexual implications of this challenge to John's household authority should not obscure the story's central emphasis on the role of African-American cultural traditions in articulating a stubborn humanitarianism against the patriarchal logic of oppression. By drawing Annie into the circle of victimhood, Julius makes it clear that the ideological boundaries that divide Chesnutt's postwar plantation are not drawn simply in black and white, and that such divisions persist in exacting a human cost, long after the official end of slavery.

"The Gray Wolf's Ha'nt"

Yet another gloomy afternoon has descended on the piazza at the beginning of "The Gray Wolf's Ha'nt."[28] John is reading a volume of philosophy and enjoying a cigar when Annie slumps into the rocking chair beside him and "petulantly" exclaims: "I wish you would talk to me, or read to me—or something." With characteristic insensitivity, he begins to read from the text in his hands:

> "The difficulty of dealing with transformations so many-sided as those which all existences have undergone, or are undergoing, is such as to make a complete and deductive interpretation almost hopeless. So to grasp the total process of redistribution of matter and motion as to see simultaneously its several necessary results in their actual interdependence is scarcely possible. There is, however, a mode of rendering the process as a whole tolerably comprehensible. Though the genesis of the rearrangement of every evolving aggregate is in itself one, it presents to our intelligence"—
> "John," interrupted my wife, "I wish you would stop reading that nonsense and see who that is coming up the lane." (*Conjure,* 95)

This interruption evokes a sigh from John, who laments over his wife's inability to entertain complex philosophical ideas. Yet the timing of Annie's impatient remark suggests that she may understand John's lifeless treatise on "the difficulty of dealing with transformations" better than he does. As Eric Selinger has pointed out, the incomplete sentence possesses unmistakable momentum in that it appears headed from an abstract conception of unity ("though the genesis ... is in itself one") toward a provisional account of multiplicity (Selinger, 679).[29] Annie abruptly puts an end to John's pedantic "nonsense" before he can explain how "our intelligence" grapples with "the redistribution of matter and motion," and her petulant tone would seem to contain one of Chesnutt's many authorial jibes at his narrator's unflappable intellectual arrogance. On the other hand, Annie's recognition of Julius approaching up the lane might be understood less as a rejection of John's arid philosophical discourse than as a completion of the text's immanent thought. Storytelling, Chesnutt hints through Julius's timely appearance, may be the "mode" through which the multiplicity of "all existences" presents itself to our intelligence, despite the hopelessness of efforts to arrive at "a complete and deductive interpretation." While John fails to realize the fact himself, his abstract philosophical text works obliquely toward a validation of Julius's art, the art of "rendering the process [of transformation] ... tolerably comprehensible."[30] It is John, the intellectually inclined husband, in other words, rather than his sentimental wife, who remains impervious to philosophy, "even when [or especially when] presented in the simplest and most lucid form" (*Conjure*, 95).

With this elaborate introduction, Julius proceeds to entertain John and Annie with a tragic story of intraracial violence, involving the lovers Dan and Mahaly. When Dan notices a conjure man's son making advances toward Mahaly, his dangerous temper takes control, and he inadvertently kills the interloper. Terrified that the conjure man will discover him, Dan appeals to Aunt Peggy for a "life cha'm" that will protect him from witchcraft (*Conjure*, 99). The two conjurers match skills against one another, until the conjure man succeeds in destroying Dan's charm, leaving him vulnerable to retribution. Having exposed his adversary, the conjure man exacts revenge by exploiting Dan's cupidity, convincing the slave that he must murder his protector to be rid of her dangerous witchcraft. To accomplish the murder, Dan consents to be transformed temporarily into a wolf, and in this disguise he lies in wait for Peggy, whom he expects to meet in the form of a black cat on her way to his cabin. As he tears fatally into its throat, the cat is transformed into Mahaly, "en Dan seed dat he had killt his own wife" (*Conjure*, 103). Having apparently accomplished his revenge, the conjure man finally offers to turn Dan back into a slave, but again Dan is duped into acting as the agent of his own destruction. Following the conjure man's instructions, he drinks a mixture that fixes his transformation forever, so that "all de conj'in in de worl' won't nebber take it off" (*Conjure*, 104).

In its representation of conjure as a vindictive force employed in the settlement of disputes within the African-American community, "The Gray Wolf's Ha'nt" echoes another story of masculine retribution, "The Conjurer's Revenge." As in Primus's tale, male jealousy results in violence between blacks, and "The Gray Wolf's Ha'nt" concludes unhappily with another failed attempt to reverse the spell of dehumanization. These details might be sufficient in themselves to explain why Annie, who at first seems so eager for a narrative alternative to John's philosophical "nonsense," remains conspicuously silent at the end of Julius's performance, leaving John to theorize about the storyteller's petty financial motives for delivering the yarn. The open distaste she expresses in "The Conjurer's Revenge" for stories depicting masculine vindictiveness and destructive intraracial rivalry is here apparently registered in a cool, unappreciative silence.

For all her neurasthenic torpor, however, Annie is not prone to withhold criticism, and her silence may convey troubled engagement with Julius's story. Conflict occurs entirely within an African-American world in "The Gray Wolf's Ha'nt," yet Annie possesses compelling reasons for drawing an imaginative parallel between Julius's account of domestic violence and her own tenuous marital situation. In light of John's repeated demonstration of insensitivity to her emotional and intellectual needs—insensitivity that borders on neglect at the beginning of this story, and that elsewhere appears to forebode some "impending misfortune"—Annie cannot help but read personal significance into the story of Mahaly's brutal victimization by a husband who fatally mistakes her identity (*Conjure*, 82). When her body is found the next day, after Dan has disappeared, the white folks " 'lowed he'd quo'lled wid Mahaly en killt her, en run erway" (*Conjure*, 105). Julius insists on another version of events, but his elaborate account of circumstances leading up to the murder only translates the gruesome domestic drama into symbolic terms. While Julius concludes by warning John that bad luck lies in store for anyone who disturbs the ghosts of Dan and Mahaly, the story may contain a more profound warning to Annie about the consequences of genteel spousal abuse.

To speculate on Annie's potential for identification with Mahaly, however, is to invest "The Gray Wolf's Ha'nt" with a rhetorical coherence the story may significantly lack. Unlike "Po' Sandy" and "Mars Jeems's Nightmare," in which Julius explicitly courts Annie's sympathy with female victims, this tale does not offer a clear parabolic link between black and white, pre- and postbellum worlds, and its failure to project such an imaginative connection may be an indication of Julius's declining effectiveness as a mouthpiece for Chesnutt's art. Pursuing this intriguing line of interpretation, Selinger alludes to the sexual potency of Julius's rabbit's foot in "Sis' Becky's Pickaninny," noting that "The Gray Wolf's Ha'nt" ends very differently by hinting at the storyteller's symbolic castration (Selinger, 683). Whereas the image of the rabbit's foot hidden in the folds of Annie's dress casts John's manhood in an uncertain light in the earlier story, here John effectively stands up to the interpretive challenge, ignoring Julius's advice against clearing "the land in question." As a consequence of his determination, John discovers not Mahaly's sunken grave, but "a bee-tree in the woods, with an ample cavity in its trunk, and an opening through which convenient access could be had to the stores of honey within" (*Conjure*, 106). If, as Selinger suggests, this honey tree is another figure for sexual potency, like the rabbit's foot, in removing it from the landscape John would appear to have won back some of his former authority, terminating Julius's "monopoly" on both the honey and Annie's attention. The very fact that the tale curiously fails to connect with its audience, evoking silence from Annie and smug approval from John, might be understood as a commentary on power relations emerging on the postwar plantation. Both here and in *The Conjure Woman*'s final story, "Hot-Foot Hannibal," Julius's narrative performances gratify white ears by focusing on conflict within the African-American community, deliberately avoiding the sort of penetrating social critique that characterizes his most compelling tales. As a result, Julius's effectiveness as a voice of resistance to patriarchal authority is noticeably diminished, and Chesnutt's powerful ironies acquire an unmistakable note of self-reproach.

"Hot-Foot Hannibal"

If the subversive capacity of Julius's art has become problematically obscure in "The Gray Wolf's Ha'nt," "Hot-Foot Hannibal" is a logical and appropriate sequel.[31] Here, for the first time, Julius delivers a story apparently without self-interest, deploying his narrative gamesmanship to settle a lovers' quarrel between Annie's sister, Mabel, and her betrothed, the "high-spirited" young Southerner Malcolm Murchison (*Conjure*, 107). As the loyal black retainer who facilitates a symbolic reconciliation between North and South, Julius assumes a highly conventional role in this tale, a role designed apparently to reassure Chesnutt's readers that for all the ex-slave's maneuvering for control within the contested postwar Southern domain, the conjure stories are finally contained within the ideological imperatives of the plantation tradition. As what Andrews has called Chesnutt's "return to orthodoxy," the story reaffirms the image of Julius's symbolic castration at the close of "The Gray Wolf's Ha'nt," implying that the old man's vernacular art, like the antebellum art of conjure, ultimately serves the interests of his employers (Andrews, 52).

Chesnutt was quite deliberate about conveying this reassuring message in *The Conjure Woman*'s final tale, which he hoped would leave "a good taste in the mouth" of his predominately white readership (Helen Chesnutt, 101). The mixed reception of his most serious work prior to the book's publication in 1899 had taught him to value George Washington Cable's advice that it is safer to indulge than to critique the prejudices of one's audience.[32] Chesnutt's dialect stories typically sustain a careful balance between indulgence and critique, offering to flatter John while leading Annie to a keener sympathy for African-American aspiration, but here the balance has apparently shifted as a concession to postbellum white fantasies of racial mastery. Nevertheless, while "Hot-Foot Hannibal" is undeniably driven by the logic of accommodation, it would be a mistake to dismiss Julius's performance as an exceptional instance of toadyism. To the contrary, the story merely bears out more cynically than any of the previous conjure tales the taut irony that operates whenever Julius speaks in Chesnutt's fiction.

John is the first to comment on the romantic crisis between Mabel and Malcolm, whose union he has supported because of its obvious social and economic advantages to himself. Exhibiting an overabundance of Northern "pride and independence," the "capricious" Mabel has broken off a match that had "promised to be another link" binding John "to the kindly Southern people" (*Conjure*, 107–8). As a further expression of the marriage between Northern capital and neglected Southern industries, the relationship between Mabel and Malcolm possesses crucial significance for John, who discusses the matter with Annie when it appears that time alone will not "heal the breach." Taking a characteristically different view of the affair, Annie notes that Malcolm bears responsibility for having said to Mabel "things ... that no woman of any spirit could stand." Up to this point, Julius's stories have typically served to instill Annie with precisely this "spirit," in defiance of John's enervating cultural authority, yet here his narrative intervention intends to reconcile the estranged lovers by convincing Mabel to swallow her pride. Accordingly, while John's mare stubbornly balks at a stream crossing, Julius entertains Annie, John, and Mabel with the story of a botched antebellum love affair between the slave Jeff and his headstrong woman, Chloe.

Chloe's troubles begin when her master, Mars Dugal' McAdoo, selects a young field hand named Hannibal to become his new houseboy, promising to let him marry Chloe if he performs his duties acceptably. Having decided that she prefers Jeff, Chloe appeals for Aunt Peggy's help in replacing Hannibal with her own love interest. Peggy supplies "a baby doll, wid a body made out'n a piece er co'n-stalk ... en a head made out'n elderberry peth, en two little red peppers fer feet," and instructs Jeff to plant the charm in the master's house, where its influence will cause Hannibal to be "light-headed en hot-footed" (*Conjure*, 112). When his clumsiness and confusion result in Mars Dugal's disfavor, Hannibal is exiled to the fields, and Jeff is installed in his place.

All goes well for the lovers until Hannibal takes revenge by exploiting Chloe's jealousy, impersonating a woman to convince her that Jeff has taken another lover. In her misguided rage, Chloe reveals the part she and Jeff have played in discrediting Hannibal, and Mars Dugal' promptly sells Jeff as a lesson to others who might invoke Peggy's conjure to interfere with his authority. When Chloe begins pining away for her lost lover, Mars Dugal' attempts to buy Jeff back, but the slave trader informs him that Jeff has taken his own life. Weeks later, Chloe's corpse is discovered "layin' in de branch yander, right 'cross fum whar we're settin' now."

> "Eber sence den," said Julius in conclusion, "Chloe's ha'nt comes eve'y ebenin' en sets down unner dat willer-tree en waits fer Jeff, er e'se walks up en down de road yander, lookin' en lookin', en waitin' en waitin', fer her sweethea't w'at ain' neber, neber come back ter her no mo'." (*Conjure*, 118)

This lugubrious conclusion evokes tears from Annie and Mabel, who identify with Chloe's lonesome suffering and are chastened by Julius's account of its source in Chloe's irrational jealousy. Apparently impressed that female "pride and independence" are a recipe for melancholy, Mabel leaves the rockaway to search for and humble herself to Malcolm, before it is too late. Julius tactfully lingers for "an unconscionably long time" while pretending to search for Annie's fan, so that when Annie and John finally encounter the young couple walking arm in arm, "their faces were aglow with the light of love" (*Conjure*, 119). John for once grasps the full significance of Julius's performance, and he takes evident pleasure in supplying its moral by noting that the mare "was never known to balk again" (*Conjure*, 120).

John's ability to provide this sexist gloss on the story's didactic purpose leaves anything but "a good taste in the mouth" of readers who have learned to relish Julius's imaginative independence and to admire his sympathetic response to Annie's suffering. Indeed, the story impresses many readers as a signal of Julius's failure as a subversive voice, and as an admission on Chesnutt's part that the dialect of resistance finally breeds compliance with the most oppressive forms of authority.[33] There is little doubt that Julius's self-effacing art has reached an outer limit in "Hot-Foot Hannibal," to the point that he seems almost to disappear in the loving glow of a North-South rapprochement made possible by his sacrificial offering of Chloe's tale.[34] The decisive losers in this uplifting story of national reconciliation, as Chesnutt knew from bitter experience, were African Americans like Julius himself, and Chesnutt may have intended to drive home a political message about misguided black complicity in arranging the regional marriage of Northern and Southern interests. But this reading assumes an unprecedented level of romantic irony in Chesnutt's conception of Julius, irony that is absent from the storyteller's highly self-conscious imaginative performances elsewhere in *The Conjure Woman*.

Rather than understand "Hot-Foot Hannibal" as an anomalous default on the promise of earlier stories like "Po' Sandy" and "Mars Jeems's Nightmare," in which Julius appears to assert a measure of creative control over his and John's environment, "Hot-Foot" should serve to qualify that promise by reminding us that Julius's narrative blend of conjure and persuasion is thoroughly and ambivalently entangled in the cultural circumstances of the postwar plantation. His capacity for resistance is always limited by his participation in a system of hierarchies that he can nudge, perhaps modify, but never escape. This is Chesnutt's great frustration with Julius as the inadequate voice of his own aspirations, and it is also the source of his subtlest rendering of the dynamics of racial mastery and humiliation in post–Civil War America. Julius's acts of resistance to John's authority always entail some measure of self-degradation, just as his humiliation is generally tinged with the spirit of defiance. Anthologizers of Chesnutt's work have understandably reproduced mainly the stories that show Julius at his best, yet to read selectively from *The Conjure Woman* is to risk idealizing the ex-slave's powers of vernacular resistance, thereby obscuring what emerges in "Hot-Foot Hannibal" as the unwelcome but, to Chesnutt, essential sense of Julius's limitation.

It is appropriate that *The Conjure Woman* closes with an ambiguously uplifting reminder of Julius's ineffectiveness as a subversive figure, for Chesnutt—not Julius—is the collection's real trickster. Chesnutt's impatience with Julius as a vehicle for his art is audible throughout the book and may culminate in a story omitted from the collection, "The Dumb Witness," in which John actually takes over Julius's role by narrating one of his coachman's tales of antebellum cruelty and retribution.[35] Julius's silence in the story's frame is an extension of Viney's mute resistance to the authority of her former lover and master, resistance she expresses in garbled tones that may be the perfect nonsense of a madwoman, or, John suspects, may represent some dialect not "of European origin" (*Conjure*, 160). This powerful story about the breakdown of communication between Viney and old Mr. Murchison thematizes Chesnutt's ambivalence about the dialect formula by disrupting the fluid narrative exchange between black and white characters, calling into question the very linguistic hierarchy on which the dialect tale depends as a form.

"Dave's Neckliss"

"The Dumb Witness" makes an intriguing companion to "Hot-Foot Hannibal," for both tales test the conceptual limits of dialect writing in the local color mode, one through its exaggerated, perhaps cynical embrace of literary convention, the other through its radical silencing of the black vernacular voice. Nevertheless, while these two stories betray Chesnutt's impatience with generic limitations imposed on his art by the exigencies of the literary marketplace, his most compelling critique of slavery and postwar peonage operates entirely within the terms of the local color tradition. "Dave's Neckliss," Chesnutt's masterpiece in the dialect mode, opens with John's lengthy ruminations on his servant's "curiously undeveloped nature."[36] Julius, according to John, was

> subject to moods which were almost childish in their variableness. It was only now and then that we were able to study, through the medium of his recollection, the simple but intensely human inner life of slavery.... While he mentioned with a warm appreciation the acts of kindness which those in authority had shown to him and his people, he would speak of a cruel deed, not with the indignation of one accustomed to quick feeling and spontaneous expression, but with a furtive disapproval which suggested to us a doubt in his own mind as to

whether he had a right to think or to feel, and presented to us the curious psychological spectacle of a mind enslaved long after the shackles had been struck off from the limbs of its possessor. (*Conjure*, 124)

John's impression of the freedman's perpetual psychological enslavement is apparently borne out in the tale. Dave is a pious and hardworking slave, until he is punished for a theft he did not commit by having a ham shackled to his neck. This token of his reification under slavery puts an end to Dave's intellectual growth—he had become literate—and destroys his standing as an organizer of the black religious community. The ham (which, as Sundquist points out, recalls the biblical Ham, progenitor of servants) operates for the master as a punitive reminder that the slave's identity is inextricably linked to his commodity status, regardless of intellectual or spiritual aspirations of the sort that originally distinguish Dave as a cultural leader (Sundquist, 382). But when Dave begins to identify too closely with the token of his degradation, becoming obsessed with hams to the point of madness, the master recognizes an imminent threat to his pocketbook and has the shackles removed. Dave's liberation is a mixed blessing, as Julius explains, for "de ham had be'n on his neck so long dat Dave had sorter got use' ter it. He look des lack he'd los' sump'n fer a day er so atter de ham wuz tuk off, en didn' 'pear to know w'at ter do wid hisse'f" (*Conjure*, 131). Unable to give up the symbol to which his identity has become firmly attached, Dave devises a pathetic substitute, tethering himself to a pine log when no one is looking to express what has become the inescapable sense of his reification. The tale concludes with a grisly pun, as Dave finally resorts to suicide in his search for a cure—in Julius's rendering, a "kyo"—for the psychological burden of enslavement. Julius comments that "Dave had kep' on gittin' wusser en wusser in his mine, 'tel he des got ter b'lievin' he wuz all done turnt ter a ham; en den he had gone en built a fier, en tied a rope roun' his neck, des lack de hams wuz tied, en had hung hisse'f up in de smoke-'ouse fer ter kyo" (*Conjure*, 134).

Robbed of his fledgling identity as a literate black man, coerced into identification with an inanimate object, then robbed again of the source of his reified slave identity, Dave is another of Chesnutt's representative postwar African Americans, a case study in the freedman's enduring psychological chaos. Like "Mars Jeems's Nightmare" and "The Conjurer's Revenge," the story suggests that freedom as a state of consciousness—"a glowing flame of sensibility" ignited by "the sacred name of liberty," in John's words—is not easily assumed by characters who have suffered the enforced dehumanization of slavery (*Conjure,* 124–25). The conjure element has been replaced in "Dave's Neckliss" by a gruesome psychological realism, with the result that this account of human transformation lacks the "Oriental," fairy-tale quality of many of Chesnutt's plantation stories.[37] But the tale unfolds along a familiar boundary between the animate and inanimate worlds and registers symbolically not only the physical and intellectual degradation of human beings in bondage, but also the problematic postwar transition from slavery to freedom. Sandy never recovers from his metamorphosis into a tree in "Po' Sandy"; Primus, the unfortunate protagonist of "The Conjurer's Revenge," remains trapped in a dual existence, half man and half mule; Dan in "The Gray Wolf's Ha'nt" is condemned to live as a wolf after his failed restoration—like Dave, each of these characters suffers a twofold human tragedy that subtly conflates the twin indignities of chattelism and Jim Crow.

Yet to read "Dave's Neckliss" as an apology for the freedman's intellectual shortcomings is to overlook Julius's investment in the story and its performance. As John suggests in his opening comments, Julius's curious narrative habit of dwelling on the antebellum past presents to the Northern couple "the curious psychological spectacle" of an imagination enslaved long after the physical shackles have been removed. John repeatedly draws this conclusion about Julius's imaginative relation to the period "befo' de wah," explaining in "Mars Jeems's Nightmare" that Julius "had been unable to break off entirely the mental habits of a lifetime" (*Conjure,* 55). In "A Victim of Heredity," John again rationalizes African-American behavior by asserting that several of his "dusky neighbors" "did not shake off readily the habits formed under the old system" (*Conjure,* 172). According to John's view, Julius's commitment to the past, expressed in stories of plantation life, confirms his intellectual and imaginative limitation, leading John to doubt that Julius "even realized, except in a vague, uncertain way, his own degradation" (*Conjure,* 125).

These astounding remarks serve to contextualize Dave's story, yet another of Julius's forays into the antebellum past. As a parable about the insufferable dilemma of a "mind enslaved long after the shackles had been struck off," the tale would seem to offer symbolic confirmation for John's beliefs, bearing out most dramatically his view of Julius and other postwar blacks as the perpetual victims of mental habits formed under slavery. Yet in telling John exactly what John already thinks he knows about his "dusky neighbors," Julius demonstrates a level of self-consciousness that is inconsistent with John's theory of mental habitude. In effect, the tale allegorizes Julius's own degradation as a legatee of the slave regime, fitting the ham-loving ex-slave neatly into a minstrel stereotype (Julius, like Dave, gazes longingly at the ham on Annie's table in a suggestive act of identification); yet in apparently embracing John's condescending explanation for African-American shortcomings in the postwar era, Julius assumes creative authority over the stereotype of the psychologically scarred and limited freedman, revealing himself to be acutely sensitive to the varieties of degradation suffered by blacks before and after the war. As Eric Sundquist cogently explains, "Dave's Neckliss" "revels in the exploration of a culturally destructive image in order to appropriate its power in an act of figurative metamorphosis. Chesnutt's fictive seizure of the image, that is to say, is itself an act of cultural conjure that reclaims and transforms its significance" (Sundquist, 381).

This "seizure" of a "culturally destructive image" is the decisive act of transformation in each of Chesnutt's tales of antebellum conjure and metamorphosis. Through his creative rendering of Dave's story, Julius inhabits the demeaning stereotype of the nostalgic ex-slave, mentally incapable of abandoning his former condition, even while he reveals the tragic attachment to stereotype as one aspect of Dave's (and his own) degradation. The story's telling, in other words, both confirms and belies John's theory of the black "appurtenance," spelled out most thoroughly in "Mars Jeems's Nightmare," where John describes Julius's persistent habit of thinking of himself as an article belonging to the plantation. Presumably like Dave, Julius simply cannot relinquish his former relation to white authority; yet his ability to narrate Dave's story—to allegorize self-consciously the tragic consequences of Dave's psychological enslavement—betrays Julius's highly cultivated performance of blackness *as* a performance.

"A Victim of Heredity"

Chesnutt's finest dialect tales resemble "Dave's Neckliss" in their complex embrace of stereotype, none more effectively than the minor masterpiece "A Victim of Heredity; or, Why the Darkey Loves Chicken."[38] The tale's overtly patronizing subtitle echoes such minstrel showstoppers as "Who Dat Say Chicken in Dis Crowd?," a popular "coon song" that plays on the exaggerated representation of African Americans as irredeemable chicken thieves (Sundquist, 380). Julius narrates the story apparently to bear out his assertion that an appetite for chicken is "in the blood" of African Americans, who ought to be afforded "mo' lowance" for petty crimes committed out of hereditary compulsion. As in "Mars Jeems's Nightmare," where Julius cites "nachul bawn laz'ness" as the reason for his grandson's irresponsibility, here he embraces the minstrel characterization of African Americans as naturally disposed to shiftless gluttony, arguing that "cullud folks is mo' fonder er chick'n 'n w'ite folks" because "dey can't he'p but be" (*Conjure*, 58, 174). Annie responds angrily to this demeaning account of African-American cultural difference, exclaiming "with some show of indignation" that Julius "ought to be ashamed to slander [his] race in that way" (*Conjure*, 174). Yet her indignation is characteristically overstated, for Annie fails to grasp Julius's probing critique of the minstrel logic his tale deploys for its own purposes.

Much like "The Goophered Grapevine," the story revolves around an acquisitive master's self-defeating effort to increase his wealth through the intervention of conjure into the plantation economy. Mars Donal' pays Aunt Peggy for a goopher mixture that will control the appetite of his slaves so that he can cut their rations without objection. He is so impressed with his success, however, that he applies a catastrophic second dose, reducing his slaves to invalids. As a convalescent measure, Aunt Peggy recommends a steady diet of chicken, which Mars Donal' provides at ruinous expense to himself. Peggy finally concocts an antidote that will restore the appetite of his slaves, but not before Mars Donal' has squandered his wealth. Moreover, she explains that the goopher was applied so carelessly that "its got in dey blood ... [s]o I 'spec's you'll hatter gib yo' niggers chick'n at leas' oncet a week ez long ez dey libs, ef you wanter git de wuk out'n 'em dat you oughter" (*Conjure*, 181). Julius concludes by theorizing that

> dey wuz so many niggers on ole Mars Donal's plantation ... en dey got scattered roun' so befo' de wah en sence, dat dey ain' ha'dly no cullu'd folks in No'f Ca'lina but w'at's got some er de blood er dem goophered niggers in dey vames. En so eber sence den, all de niggers in No'f Ca'lina has ter hab chick'n at leas' oncet er week fer ter keep dey healt' en strenk. En dat's w'y cullu'd folks laks chick'n mo' d'n w'ite folks. (*Conjure*, 181)

Rather than argue for the innate equality of the races by rooting out an offensive cultural fiction, Julius demands that the minstrel representation of the African-American chicken thief is thoroughly inscribed "in the blood." Annie initially objects to the degrading logic of this plea for leniency, just as she upbraids Julius for his apparent self-deprecation in "The Conjurer's Revenge." But Annie's egalitarian instincts are misguided here, for Julius insists on the "influence of heredity" as a way of appropriating a racist caricature in order to redirect its cultural significance. The strategy is a familiar one: Julius's tale gratifies John's worst assumptions about African-American inferiority by arguing that blacks are naturally compelled to steal chicken, at whatever risk to themselves; but this "natural" disposition, according to the tale, is entirely due to environmental conditions linked to slavery and racism. While Aunt Peggy's goopher is forever dispersed in the blood of ex-slaves, leaving them uniquely susceptible to criminal temptations, Mars Donal' is the one responsible for putting it there. Thus despite the story's offensively reductive account of African-American racial traits inherited from the era "befo' de wah," heredity and environment are finally interchangeable and indistinguishable terms. The stereotype may be "in the blood," according to Julius's parable, but only in the sense that black blood is part of a much larger cultural fiction constructed by whites to serve the needs of oppression. Much like Booker T. Washington, who examines chicken stealing as a potent cultural metaphor in *Up from Slavery,* Julius employs a demeaning self-representation to subvert racist assumptions that underlie its use.[39]

"Tobe's Tribulations"

Julius's strategic embrace of stereotype typically operates as a veiled critique of coercive practices employed by members of Mars Donal's master class, but the dialect stories occasionally launch a very different sort of critique. One of Chesnutt's most remarkable tales, "Tobe's Tribulations," for example, takes its slave protagonist to task for failing to grasp the full significance of freedom. When Tobe queries Aunt Peggy about the easiest way to reach the North, she raises a question to which he cannot frame a compelling reply: "W'at you wanter be free fer?" (*Conjure,* 187). He admits that conditions on the plantation are bearable but contends that life in the North will afford better food and more sleep.[40] Finally, Tobe explains that although he isn't expected to work too hard "fer a slabe nigger," "ef I wuz free I wouldn' wuk a-tall 'less'n I felt lak it." Chesnutt's rigorous work ethic and commitment to the principle of self-improvement may be audible in Aunt Peggy's discouraging reply: " 'I

dunno, nigger ... whuther you gwine fin' w'at you er huntin' fer er no.' "
She advises him to follow the North Star, "en den maybe in a mont' er so
you'll retch de Norf en you'll be free, en whar you kin eat all you want, ef
you kin git it, en sleep ez long ez you mineter, ef you kin 'ford it, en whar
you won't hafter wuk ef you'd ruther go to jail" (*Conjure*, 187).

Aunt Peggy might be interpreted here as arguing that Tobe is better
off under the paternalistic authority of a Southern master than he would
be in the free North, and indeed Chesnutt (like Dunbar) has been
accused of taking an accommodationist stand on the important question
of black emigration to Northern cities in the post-Reconstruction era.[41]
The nondialect story "Uncle Wellington's Wives," like "Dave's Neckliss," treads perilously close to such a position on the freedman's readi-
ness to assume the liberties represented by the North Star, which the
protagonist of that story ironically keeps over his shoulder as he flees
the North in search of friendlier Southern skies. But to understand
Chesnutt as an apologist for Southern paternalism is to obscure his
vision of racial justice. Tobe's tribulations result not from his misguided
desire for freedom, but as a consequence of his failure to desire freedom
profoundly enough. As Aunt Peggy warns, again sounding much like
Chesnutt himself: "I'se feared you wants ter git free too easy" (*Conjure*,
187). Laziness and a lack of self-respect are the twin sources of Tobe's
eventual failure to complete the psychological transition from slavery to
freedom. Like so many of Chesnutt's characters, including Dave, Sandy,
Primus, and others, he is left in that ambiguous liminal state between
animal and man, slave and freedman, a figure for Chesnutt's representative postwar African American.

Thanks to an accidental overdose of Aunt Peggy's goopher, Tobe
enjoys a comfortable if uncertain existence as a frog, a condition perfectly suited to his vision of freedom as limitless leisure. Nevertheless,
having symbolically dodged Southern slavery and Northern poverty,
Tobe is threatened with a new sort of exploitation as the story opens. In
his characteristic role as the harbinger of a new economic order, John
entertains the idea of harvesting the swamp for edible frogs, reintro-
ducing the specter of commodification in the postwar era. If Tobe's
"batrachian" disguise can be taken as symbolic of the freedman's condition more generally, as Sundquist has argued, then John's plan to harvest
frogs "as a source of food-supply" takes on special significance for Julius,
who concludes Tobe's story with the recommendation that this unfortunate ex-slave "oughter be 'lowed ter lib out de res' er his days in

peace" (*Conjure*, 184, 192).[42] Unable to appreciate the significance of
freedom, incapable of returning to his former state as a plantation slave,
Tobe—like Julius—merely hangs on, croaking soulfully in concert with
his fellow frogs. The story's critique moves in two directions at once,
focusing on Tobe's inadequate energy and on John's opportunistic
appetite, suggesting that both are responsible for the freedman's incomplete assumption of the rights and liberties of full citizenship.

"Lonesome Ben"

John's efforts to develop another neglected plantation resource again
inspire Julius to narrate a tale of unsuccessful flight in "Lonesome
Ben."[43] As in "Dave's Neckliss," the conjure element has been replaced
by a harrowing psychological realism in this symbolic account of an
escaped slave's acute alienation. The story opens as John and Annie are
examining several clay banks along the branch in search of a suitable
source for brick. On their way, the Northern couple passes the house of
a farmhand, and John remarks that the woman of the house bears a complexion of "ruddy brown," tinged with a "sickly hue." "Indeed," he continues, "I had observed a greater sallowness among both the colored
people and the poor whites thereabouts than the hygienic conditions of
the neighborhood seemed to justify" (*Conjure*, 146–47). While John,
Annie, and Julius wait beside the branch for Mabel to pass by, "a white
woman wearing a homespun dress and slat-bonnet" appears by the
water and secretively gathers a ball of clay. When Annie asks Julius to
explain the curious spectacle, he asserts that the woman plans to eat the
clay, and adds: "I doan min' w'at dem kinder folks does ... but w'eneber
I sees black folks eat'n clay of'n dat partic'lar clay-bank, it alluz sets me
ter studyin' 'bout po' lonesome Ben" (*Conjure*, 148).

As its introductory frame obliquely suggests, "Lonesome Ben" is a
complicated tale about racial blending, "mulatto" identity, and typolo-
gies of color in the post-Reconstruction South. Ben is "one er dese yer
big black niggers ... mo' d'n six foot high an' black ez coal" (*Conjure*,
149). When he is compelled to flee Mars Marrabo's plantation because
of an imminent whipping, however, Ben's racial identity undergoes a
disorienting change. Unable to follow the star of freedom north because
of cloudy weather, he walks in circles for days after his escape and finds
himself a week later on his old plantation. Rather than turn himself in,
he hides in the woods by the branch, "slippin' out nights an' gittin' clay

ter eat an' water 'fom de crick yander ter drink. The water in dat crick wuz cl'ar in dem days," Julius adds, underlining the story's color symbolism, "stidder bein' yallar lak it is now" (*Conjure*, 151).

After subsisting on a steady diet of clay for a month, Ben sees his wife Dasdy approaching along the road and calls to her. "I never seed yer befor' in my life," she replies, "an' nebber wants ter see yer ag'in.... Whose nigger is yer? Er is yer some low-down free nigger dat doan b'long ter nobody an' doan own nobody?" (*Conjure*, 152). As Dasdy's comments imply, Ben's uncertain new economic status as neither slave nor freedman complicates his identity, leaving him suspended in an unrecognizable limbo. After his son also fails to recognize him, a fellow slave from the plantation, Primus, passes Ben on the road and greets him politely. When Ben fails to respond, Primus petulantly exclaims, "Youer de mos' mis'able lookin' merlatter I eber seed. Dem rags look lak dey be'n run th'oo a sawmill. My marster doan 'low no strange niggers roun' dis yer plantation, an' yo' better take yo' yaller hide 'way f'um yer as fas' as yo' kin" (*Conjure*, 153).

Primus's appearance in the tale is suggestive, for as the unfortunate slave who remains trapped in a dual existence at the end of "The Conjurer's Revenge," he signifies the dilemma of "mulatto" identity. Moreover, Primus's remarks contain an allusion to poor Sandy, whose name also links his demise at the sawmill to the issue of racial blending. Accordingly, Ben's incomplete transition from slavery to freedom entails a traumatic loss of identity, expressed in the iconography of color as a partial lightening of the skin. His constant ingestion of "yellowish-white" clay, according to the tale, has turned his coal-black skin into a "clay-cullud hide," a transformation that denotes Ben's emerging economic status as a man whom "nobody didn' 'pear ter wanter own" and that also spells his doom (*Conjure*, 153). Cast off by his wife, his child, his friend, and finally by his master, Ben develops a profound sense of alienation, to the point that he eventually comes to feel "mo' lak a stranger" than like himself (*Conjure*, 156). After his death beside the branch, the sun bakes his corpse into an enormous brick—like the ham, a token of absolute reification—which is later crushed by a falling tree and washed into the stream. Julius explains that the water has borne a yellow tint ever since.

It is tempting to read Ben's tale as a celebration of the master/slave relation, in that the story locates Ben's identity in his status as a coal-black slave, implying that any other identity is ultimately untenable. Ben finally goes mad not when his wife and child deny him, but when

Mars Marrabo turns away in disgust, calling him a "yellow rascal" (*Conjure*, 154). In a passage that precisely conveys the logic of the plantation tradition, Julius comments that Ben had "be'n willin ernuff to git 'long widout a marster, w'en he had one, but it 'peared lak a sin fer his own marster ter 'ny 'im an' cas' 'im off dat-a-way" (*Conjure*, 154–55). Like "Tobe's Tribulations," the story appears to valorize the bond between master and slave, suggesting that Ben would have been more content to remain in his former condition than to risk the loss of his slave identity by attempting to escape.

But the story really offers Ben no such choice at all and registers instead the psychological burden of mixed-race identity in a culture that can see only black and white. As a slave belonging to Mars Marrabo, Ben's imminent dehumanization under the whip is certain; as an ostensibly free "merlatter," living in the American South, his transformation into a thing is more protracted but no less certain. Chesnutt's thoughts about his own impossible status as a mixed-race Southerner—"too 'stuck up' for the colored folks, and, of course, not recognized by the whites"—resonate clearly in Ben's sense of alienation and displacement, which receives its most economical expression in the refrain of a bullfrog who witnesses Ben's demise: "Turnt ter clay! Turnt ter clay! Turnt ter clay!" (*Conjure*, 155). When John picks up on these words, quoting from *Hamlet* ("Imperious Caesar, turned to clay, / Might stop a hole to keep the wind away"), Julius points out that the lines are not quite appropriate, for "it wuz Ben, you 'member, not Caesar. Ole Mars Marrabo did hab a nigger name' Caesar, but dat wuz anudder one" (*Conjure*, 155–56). With this understated qualification of John's literary allusion, Julius insists on the culturally specific nature of Ben's dilemma as an invisible man on the Southern plantation.

The tale of Ben's transition from a coal-black slave into a free "merlatter," and of his consequent loss of a recognizable identity, casts some light on the story's opening scene, including John's observation of a curious "sallowness among both the colored people and the poor whites" in the neighborhood. As Julius explains, poverty-stricken whites and blacks occasionally feed on the edible clay, with the result that the skin of both groups has come to acquire a uniform "rather sickly hue." The New South, Chesnutt implies, while it clings to fictitious paradigms of identity, is no longer black or white but is rather a complex blend of different shades, like the stream that runs through John's plantation. Clay-eating by members of both races in the story is a metaphor for racial amalgamation, or miscegenation, the blending of physical and cultural characteristics that lies behind Chesnutt's master trope of the new Southern grapevine, knotted and twined in an inevitable cultural synthesis. Julius's storytelling, like Chesnutt's art more generally, is the self-conscious product of just such a synthesis, as John observes in a rare moment of insight when he describes the old man's tales as emerging out of a combination of "ancestral fetishism" and Scotch superstition, Africa and Europe "filtered" through the storyteller's imagination (*Conjure*, 185). This cultural blending, of which conjure itself is a product, comes at a terrific risk to established structures of identity, as Julius's stories constantly emphasize, yet the image of the yellow stream that was once "cl'ar," or of the tangled grapevine that was once Mars Dugal's perfect monopoly, represents Chesnutt's most profound social vision for America after Reconstruction.

For all his artful subversion of social and economic relations that threaten to disrupt this vision, Julius can only hint symbolically at its possibility, and this may be Chesnutt's greatest frustration with the asymmetrical pattern of dialect fiction. While his stories consistently reveal the "intensely human inner life of slavery," as John puts it in "Dave's Neckliss," they begin and end with an affirmation of stark intellectual inequality, an affirmation inscribed in the very linguistic differences that clearly mark Julius as an illiterate speaker (*Conjure*, 124). Moreover, the permanent discontinuity between John's latinate, bourgeois idiom and Julius's earthy black dialect implicitly nullifies the very range of social possibilities that the stories ostensibly seek to open up, social possibilities that exist somewhere between John's and Julius's mutually exclusive worlds, in a cultural space the dialect tales can only vaguely suggest. Rather than disrupt the balance of power implied by their linguistic differences, Julius's stories typically serve to invigorate John and Annie by diverting them from their spiritually deadening routine. Understood as entertainment, the tales thus incur a significant cost for their limited subversive gains. Julius, according to Richard Brodhead, "is giving up his people's life as other people's entertainment. Like a long line of black show business successes in American white culture he wins an enhanced social place for himself by making African-American expressive forms and 'soul' available to others' imaginative participation and consumption" (*Conjure*, 12).

In the finest of his Uncle Julius stories, including "The Goophered Grapevine," "Po' Sandy," "Mars Jeems's Nightmare," and "Dave's Neckliss," Chesnutt demonstrates an unparalleled artistry in imagining the empowerment of African Americans under massively limiting physical and intellectual conditions. Personally, however, he shared little in common with the vernacular protagonists whose humanity he insistently described in tales of madness and magical transformation. The real subject of his imaginative work, Chesnutt believed, lay in the representation of a social reality obscured by the dialect formula, even in its most subversive mood, a social reality never before explored in American literature. In his second story collection, *The Wife of His Youth and Other Stories of the Color Line*, he succeeded at last in addressing a predominately white American audience on his own terms, challenging accepted stereotypes of African-American character and behavior not by inhabiting them, like Julius, but by disclosing credible alternatives that exist within the complex milieu of the color line.

The Nondialect Stories

Musing about his abbreviated literary career in 1928, more than 25 years after the decision to reopen his lucrative stenography business, Chesnutt described the focus of his imaginative work in the following way:

> My physical makeup was such that I knew the psychology of people of mixed blood in so far as it differed from that of other people, and most of my writing ran along the color line.... It has more dramatic possibilities than life within clearly differentiated groups. This was perfectly natural and I have no apologies to make for it.[44]

This important comment helps to clarify Chesnutt's understanding of what was most significant about his art, and underlines again his ambivalence about the Uncle Julius stories. The dialect tales, for all their subtle resistance to the ideology of the plantation tradition, deal primarily with the lives of "widely differentiated groups," as the strictly hierarchical linguistic exchanges between John and Julius constantly emphasize. Figures who embody "the psychology of ... mixed blood" in the dialect tales— Primus and Ben may be the most memorable—are inevitably trapped in a perplexing anonymity, suspended between irreconcilable racial and cultural possibilities that leave their identities tragically uncertain.

As Chesnutt surely recognized, his characterization of such desperate "mulatto" figures was strangely consistent with the representation of the "tragic mulatto" in popular American fiction. This pervasive stereotype expressed a complicated set of assumptions about racial integrity and moral obligation, but purveyors of the stereotype—including Harriet Beecher Stowe, Mark Twain, Albion Tourgée, George Washington Cable, among many others—were clear on at least one point: that the "mulatto" or "mulatta" figure, as hero, heroine, or villain, constituted a cultural anomaly whose story inevitably resulted in sentimental or melodramatic tragedy.

Chesnutt had encountered thinking of this sort early in his career, when Richard Watson Gilder rejected the "realism" of "Rena Walden" on the grounds that the story's mixed-race characters were, in effect, not tragic enough. Gilder had complained about Rena's "amorphous" personality and "lack of spontaneous imaginative life," criticism of the sort that may have encouraged Chesnutt to cultivate the sentimental and tragic potential of his mixed-race characters along more conventional lines in the dialect stories (Helen Chesnutt, 56–59). But this concession to popular taste in the representation of mixed-race identity troubled Chesnutt deeply. He understood that for all Julius's symbolic gestures toward an image of cultural synthesis, the dialect tales tend to obscure rather than to illuminate the reality of "mulatto" existence in post-Reconstruction America, hinting only obliquely at the complexities of contemporary life along the color line. The original intention of his art, as he had outlined its "high, holy purpose" in an 1880 journal entry, had been "to accustom the public mind to the idea" of "the negro's . . . social recognition and equality" (*Journal,* 139–40). This goal could be accomplished only by breaking with the dialect formula in order to portray African-American characters "whose moral standards and social goals," according to William Andrews, "could not be reduced to those of the tragic mulatto and mulatta."[45] In his three published novels and many nondialect stories, therefore, Chesnutt dropped the vernacular plantation tale as his model and sought instead to represent the moral, social, and economic challenges facing Americans like himself in the years after slavery, always striving to prepare public opinion for the social recognition of African Americans by registering the dignity and humanity of the freedman's plight.

"The Wife of His Youth"

Ironically, while the slave past is not, as it was for Julius, the explicit subject of the nondialect stories, the freedman's relation to his past remains a central issue in Chesnutt's effort to articulate viable models of postwar African-American identity. Julius's persistent nostalgia, with its ambiguous indication of "a mind enslaved" long after the shackles had been removed, represents one version of the postwar African-American relation to the past; the color line stories, with their focus on bourgeois urban life in the postwar North, tend to replace Julius's nostalgia (including its verbal equivalent, slave dialect) with an equally problematic syndrome: what might be called repression. The classic expression of this condition comes in "The Wife of His Youth," first published in the *Atlantic Monthly* during the summer of 1898, and then reprinted the following year as the title story of Chesnutt's second and last collection of short fiction, *The Wife of His Youth and Other Stories of the Color Line.*

While Julius's imagination can be characterized by its absorption in past relations, which "clung to his mind, like barnacles to the submerged portion of a ship," the central character in this story, Mr. Ryder, has effectively banished all traces of his Southern past from consciousness (*Conjure*, 185). As a leading member of Groveland's exclusive mixed-race society of "Blue Veins," Ryder shares the group's idealized conception of whiteness and, while not a founding member himself, emerges as the society's principal custodian of "standards" based entirely on skin color (*Wife*, 3). His "genius for social leadership" facilitates the massive repression of all that the group "collectively disclaimed," namely blackness and the legacy of African-American slavery (*Wife*, 3). Ryder's pursuit of a racial fantasy, expressed in his admiration for Tennyson's "A Dream of Fair Women," promises to culminate with his marriage to Mrs. Dixon, a woman who is "whiter than he and better educated" (*Wife*, 5). Their union, he reasons, will further guarantee his eventual "absorption by the white race," a process he defends with an ironic allusion to the Great Emancipator: " 'With malice towards none, with charity for all,' we must do the best we can for ourselves and those who are to follow us. Self-preservation is the first law of nature" (*Wife*, 7).

Before he can realize his dream, however, Ryder is faced with a moral and psychological dilemma when the long-forgotten wife of his youth—a diminutive, "very black" woman—appears in search of her husband, whom she describes as "a merlatter man by de name er Sam Taylor" (*Wife*, 10–11). Recognizing her as the woman he married down South before the war and prior to his personal transformation, Ryder debates whether to pursue his dream of absorption by the white race or to acknowledge and reclaim a repressed aspect of his past. At a lavish dinner party, intended to celebrate his proposal to Mrs. Dixon, he presents the issue as a hypothetical question to his fellow Blue Veins, dropping into a "soft dialect, which came readily to his lips," to deliver Liza Jane's tale (*Wife*, 20). As if collectively awakened from their pursuit of a false ideal, the dinner guests react with a "responsive thrill" to Ryder's narration, unanimously joining Mrs. Dixon in affirming the husband's responsibility to his past (*Wife*, 20). Having evidently reached the same decision himself, Ryder happily accepts the group's verdict and acknowledges Liza Jane as the wife of his youth.

With its unambiguous moral choice and heavy-handed satire of color prejudice among middle-class African Americans, "The Wife of His Youth" undeniably possesses the flavor of a Sunday school instructional tract. To appreciate its intricate engagement with issues central to

Chesnutt's creative project, it is necessary to read the story against the context of the Uncle Julius tales, in which Chesnutt also explores the functions of cultural memory. Julius, of course, impresses John as a study in arrested intellectual development, in that his mind cannot accustom itself to altered arrangements of authority in the postwar era. Indeed, his stories constantly allegorize the difficulty of achieving a smooth transition from bondage to freedom. Presumably like Dave, Chesnutt's most wrenching example of a psychological predicament that might be explained as a crippling excess of cultural memory, Julius is wedded to a degrading antebellum image of himself as an "appurtenance" on the old plantation, a figure whose mentality, according to John, is akin to that of horses and dogs also belonging to the property (*Conjure,* 55).

Self-serving and misguided as John's opinions about his "dusky neighbors" tend to be, his psychological portrait of Julius contains one of Chesnutt's central insights into the postwar African-American context, and it is within this context that Ryder's moral dilemma takes on intriguing significance. As a character who has so successfully negotiated the transition to a new identity that he does not at first even recognize his former wife, the token of his own Southern past, Ryder constitutes Dave's and Julius's psychological antithesis. Whereas Dave—through Julius's highly motivated narration—presents the degraded "spectacle of a mind enslaved," Ryder exemplifies a different kind of degradation, for Chesnutt one no less profound, which occurs when identity becomes perfectly detached from cultural sources and communal relations. Unflattering as the comparison must seem to Liza Jane, she performs exactly the same function as the ham in "Dave's Neckliss," offering a point of reference for the protagonist's developing postwar identity. Dave is destroyed by his perfect identification with the symbol of his reification under slavery, while Ryder is quite differently threatened by his perfect detachment from a former identity, that of "a merlatter man by de name er Sam Taylor." Chesnutt implies through Dave's suicide and Ryder's enobling choice that the African-American past, with its strong cultural residue of slavery, is an essential yet potentially overwhelming component in the structure of postwar black identity.

The most poignant moment in Ryder's recovery of a cultural past occurs when he narrates Liza Jane's story to the Blue Veins, a group defined by its rejection of everything she stands for.[46] Though he is a man of "decidedly literary tastes," who has cultivated a passion for poetry along with other affectations of bourgeois respectability, Ryder drops into a "soft dialect" when he narrates Liza Jane's story, and it is his language as much as his sentimentalism that evokes "a responsive thrill in many hearts" (*Wife*, 4, 20). This is a significant detail, given Chesnutt's frustration with the dialect formula and his desire to write a more "realistic," nondialect fiction. "There were some present who had seen," the narrator explains, "and others who had heard their fathers and grandfathers tell, the wrongs and sufferings of this past generation, and all of them still felt, in their darker moments, the shadow hanging over them" (*Wife*, 20). Ryder here adopts Julius's role as a traditional vernacular storyteller, and his ministrations in this capacity help to awaken the Blue Veins to a renewed sense of communal identity. In other words, the dialect tale, even within the context of Chesnutt's deliberate move to nondialect fiction, provides the group's conduit to a disinherited past. Just as storytelling reveals Julius to be less a victim of mental habitude in the present than he pretends to be, Ryder's descent into slave legend and black vernacular establishes a healthy imaginative connection between past and present, restoring his fractured identity and the communal purpose of the Blue Veins in the process.

"The Sheriff's Children"

Chesnutt enjoyed poking fun at characters like Mr. Ryder and Cicero Clayton, the protagonist of "A Matter of Principle," mixed-race Americans who struggle somewhat pathetically to carve out a viable identity by cultivating forms of cultural amnesia. Whereas Ryder recovers his past in a moment of insight, Clayton isolates himself and his family by carrying the "principle" of white superiority to laughable, self-defeating excess. Benighted by color consciousness, snobs like Clayton and Professor Revels of "The Sway-Backed House" generally prove to be well-intentioned bigots in Chesnutt's nondialect tales, their brand of racism producing more comedy than tragedy. Chesnutt's mood is noticeably more sombre, however, when he approaches the issue of responsibility to the past from the other side of the color line, as in "The Sheriff's Children."[47]

Sheriff Campbell of Branson County, North Carolina, is, like Mr. Ryder, a character who so successfully represses elements of his past that he fails to recognize his "mulatto" son, a "wayward spirit" who returns "from the vanished past" at the beginning of the story (*Wife*, 91). As in "The Wife of His Youth," the arrival of this forgotten representative of antebellum race relations forces a crisis in the lives of characters who are apparently successfully engaged in negotiating a new social order. Torn between his commendable sense of responsibility to the principle of law and his incipient sense of duty to a mistreated son, Campbell experiences an epiphany of racial understanding in the story's climax. As his son holds a gun to the sheriff's head, the latter enjoys "a kind of clarifying of the moral faculty, in which the veil of the flesh, with its obscuring passions and prejudices, is pushed aside for a moment, and all the acts of life stand out, in the clear light of truth" (*Wife*, 90). This passage conveys a moment of insight that significantly never occurs in the dialect fiction, where John and Julius spar continually and unproductively over plantation resources. In a "clearness of spirit" inspired by the threat of racial violence, a threat John never faces in *The Conjure Woman*, the Sheriff comes to understand that he "owed some duty to this son of his—that neither law nor custom could destroy a responsibility inherent in the nature of mankind" (*Wife*, 91).

Chesnutt's highest aspiration as a writer was to produce the conditions for such a "clarifying of the moral faculty" in his audience, and indeed "The Sheriff's Children" begs to be read as an allegory of the author's strained relation to his reading public. After the "veil of flesh" has been removed from the Sheriff's moral vision, "his anger against the mulatto died away, and in its place there sprang up a great pity" (*Wife*, 91). With its open dramatization of precisely the "moral revolution" Chesnutt hoped his own art would ignite, "The Sheriff's Children" is one of the author's frankest stories, and also one of his darkest (*Journals*, 140). After Campbell has made the decision to fulfill his responsibility as a father, in defiance of social custom, he finds the "mulatto" cold and stiff on the jail floor, having bled to death during the night. It may already be too late, the story finally implies, for a transcendent vision of racial justice.

"Her Virginia Mammy"

While "The Wife of His Youth" and "The Sheriff's Children" reveal Chesnutt in two very different moods, both stories insist on the moral necessity of recognizing "the vanished past" in the present, an imaginative gesture Chesnutt clearly linked to the all-important goal of "social recognition and equality" for African Americans in the postwar era (*Journals*, 140). Straightforward as Ryder's and Campbell's dilemma might seem, however, the choice in favor of recognition is not always so clear, as Chesnutt demonstrates in another compelling account of the return of the repressed, "Her Virginia Mammy."[48] This ambiguous story describes Clara Hohlfelder's search for a secure identity. Orphaned as a child, Clara was raised by kind German immigrants who supplied her needs but could not shed light on the mystery of her origin. Her foster parents treat Clara well, but she suspects that "there is warmer, richer blood coursing in my veins than the placid stream that crept through theirs" (*Wife*, 30). Afraid that she may possess a disreputable anscestry, Clara dodges the marriage proposals of her lover, Dr. Winthrop, a Mayflower descendant whose social standing she refuses to jeopardize until the secret of her past can be known. Convinced that they both can live happily in ignorance of her past, Winthrop borrows a page from Cicero Clayton and the Blue Veins, preaching a sermon on the irrelevance of her personal history: "Dearest, ... put aside these unwholesome fantasies. Your past is shrouded in mystery. Take my name, as you have taken my love, and I'll make your future so happy that you won't have time to think of the past" (*Wife*, 31).

Chesnutt generally treats this argument as a red herring and an obstacle to the social recognition of African Americans, whose history of oppression he considered an essential component in the case for racial justice. Should Clara's mixed-race heritage be revealed and her cultural relation to an African-American community established, or should she "be able to enjoy the passing moment," as Winthrop unwittingly puns (*Wife*, 40)? The story seems bent on recognition when, by a remarkable coincidence, Clara reveals her troubles to Mrs. Harper, an attractive older woman "of clear olive complexion and regular features" to whom Clara bears an "indefinable likeness" (*Wife*, 41). Mrs. Harper holds the key to Clara's mystery, yet despite the strong suggestion of a maternal bond, she reveals only part of the truth, allowing Clara to claim an illustrious ancestry while remaining unconscious of the "taint" in her blood. "I knew it must be so," exclaims Clara, while Mrs. Harper restrains her emotion.[49] "I have often felt it. Blood will always tell" (*Wife*, 53).

Yet blood does not always tell, and the story appears to insist that under certain circumstances, it shouldn't. Clara's absorption into the white race is guaranteed by Mrs. Harper's tearful denial of her maternal relationship, a denial Chesnutt handles with more ambivalence than he generally affords to characters who design to advance socially by constructing false identities. "Joy and sorrow, love and gratitude" are "strangely blended" in Mrs. Harper's eyes as she observes her daughter's ascension to a false position of social prominence (*Wife*, 59). The ambivalence of Mrs. Harper's expression is also reflected in Winthrop's curious reaction to the news of his fiancée's discovery. Less sanguine than Clara, he dwells thoughtfully on the striking resemblance between the older woman and the younger one, noting the physical similarity with an expression that "caused Mrs. Harper's eyes to fall, and then glance up appealingly." Having discerned her secret, Winthrop does not take the obvious step of rejecting his lover, but instead suggestively wraps his arms around her "with an air of assured possession" (*Wife*, 59). Whether in adopting this attitude of dominance Winthrop enters into a new proprietary relation with his mixed-race lover, herself the product of a sexually exploitative master/slave relationship, is left unclear, but the story's perplexing final lines imply that Clara's assumption of a new identity is fraught with uncertain consequences.

Perhaps one way to make sense of the rejection of knowledge in "Her Virginia Mammy" is to consider that the story may have been written as a playful rejoinder to Frances E. W. Harper's *Iola Leroy*, an 1892 novel whose mixed-race heroine faces a predicament similar to Clara Hohlfelder's. When Dr. Gresham, the scion of a prominent New England family, proposes to the beautiful, fair-skinned Iola, she rejects his love to fulfill her duty toward her mother's black relations in the South. Chesnutt may be signifying on Harper's melodramatic novel when he describes Clara's remarkably implausible discovery of her long-lost mother, and he may be rewriting Harper's sentimental ending when he thwarts the ultimate reunion of mother and daughter to permit Clara's social advancement. Dr. Winthrop, unlike Dr. Gresham, overcomes his mixed-race lover's abstract racial allegiance to people she has never met, and "Mrs. Harper's story"—as Chesnutt coyly describes the mother's tale in "Her Virginia Mammy"—thus results in a blurring rather than a fixing of the color line.

"The Passing of Grandison"

The suppression of knowledge about racial origins serves as a catalyst to plot development in several of Chesnutt's nondialect stories, including "Cicely's Dream" and "White Weeds," both of which complicate popular assumptions about racial characteristics by withholding information concerning bloodlines and family history. Chesnutt employs a more familiar strategy to accomplish similar didactic ends in the trickster narrative, "The Passing of Grandison," which revisits the plantation setting to challenge the stereotype of the loyal black retainer.[50] As in the dialect stories, the source of confusion in "The Passing of Grandison" is the master's assumption that he understands what motivates his slaves. Colonel Owens, according to the narrator, "had pronounced views on the subject of negroes, having studied them, as he often said, for a great many years, and, as he asserted oftener still, understanding them perfectly" (*Wife*, 176–77). At the heart of the colonel's theory of African-American character lies a feudal image of the "blissful relationship" between master and slave, a relationship that entails "kindly protection on the one hand" and "wise subordination and loyal dependence on the other" (*Wife*, 179).

When he refuses to escape to the North despite the urging and abetment of the colonel's trifling son, Grandison at first appears to confirm the stereotype of the servile black dependent who is grateful for his bondage. In the story's most amusing narrative detail, the slave actually escapes the clutches of Northern abolitionists, "keeping his back steadily to the North Star" as he makes his way "back to the old plantation, back to his master, his friends, and his home" (*Wife*, 199). The tongue-in-cheek quality of this homage to plantation mythology becomes explicit only at the end of the story, when Grandison disappears with his entire extended family, and the narrator comments that "strangely enough, the underground railroad seemed to have had its tracks cleared and signals set for this particular train" (*Wife*, 201).

"The Passing of Grandison" is admittedly somewhat formulaic and predictable, but the story takes on added interest when it is compared with Mark Twain's tremendously popular *Adventures of Huckleberry Finn*, which had appeared in 1885. As a young Southerner engaged in an elaborate and insincere game of emancipation, Dick Owens bears a striking resemblance to Tom Sawyer, who orchestrates the liberation of an already free slave for his own entertainment and aggrandizement in the controversial "evasion scene" at the end of Twain's classic novel. Moreover, Grandison's inverted escape from the North to the South resembles Jim's ironic drift down the Mississippi, where freedom becomes an increasingly abstract possibility. Although Chesnutt knew Mark Twain's work and envied his popularity, it is unlikely that he was responding directly to Twain's ambivalent handling of African-American stereotypes in "The Passing of Grandison"; nevertheless, Chesnutt's uniquely subversive rendering of the racial dynamics surrounding Grandison's mock escape has the potential to infuse the ongoing debate over *Huckleberry Finn*'s purported racism with a fascinating contemporary perspective.

"The Doll"

The disappearance of Grandison's entourage comes very close to shattering Colonel Owens's "faith in sable humanity," which is grounded in an image of black docility and "servile virtue" (*Wife*, 200). Sheriff Campbell is similarly disillusioned when his prisoner seizes a gun after the sheriff "had relied on the negro's cowardice and subordination in the presence of an armed white man as a matter of course" (*Wife*, 81). Chesnutt sought to challenge the widely accepted assumption of black docility in a number of ways, often by deploying trickster inversions of the sort that occur in "The Passing of Grandison" and occasionally by depicting armed resistance to racist oppression, as in *The Marrow of Tradition*. Perhaps Chesnutt's most thoughtful rebuke of popular assumptions regarding black servility appears in a late story, "The Doll," which describes a remarkable confrontation between Colonel Forsyth, a Southern politician, and Tom Taylor, the black proprietor of a successful Northern barber shop.[51] To demonstrate his theory that blacks "are born to serve and to submit," Forsyth enters Taylor's barber shop and deliberately baits the man who holds a razor to his throat (*Stories*, 406). Maintaining that African Americans "will neither resent an insult, nor defend a right, nor avenge a wrong," the colonel proceeds to boast about his cold-blooded murder of a man who turns out to have been Taylor's father. The barber's rage mounts as he recalls his father's deathbed version of the story,

> while under his keen razor lay the neck of his enemy, the enemy, too, of his race, sworn to degrade them, to teach them, if need be, with the torch and with the gun, that their place was at the white man's feet, his heel upon their neck.... One stroke of the keen blade, a deflection of half an inch in its course, and a murder would be avenged, an enemy destroyed! (*Stories*, 409)

Both Colonel Forsyth and Tom Taylor are thinly drawn caricatures embodying stark positions in the debate over what Forsyth pejoratively calls "the Negro question," and the intensity of their confrontation is certainly overdone (*Stories*, 405). But Chesnutt is less interested in the personalities involved than in the broad symbolic implications of the encounter between an unregenerate racist and a rising middle-class black man. Describing Taylor's effort to contain his "homicidal impulse," the narrator contends that the struggle was between "society and self, civilization and the primitive instinct, typifying, more fully than the barber could realize, the great social problem involved in the future of his race" (*Stories*, 411).

In his nondialect stories Chesnutt often lapses into this instructional voice, a habit that would be more annoying if not for the presence of subtle details that frequently complicate the narrator's avowed didactic purpose. At the conclusion of this story, for example, Taylor manages to overcome his rage by remembering his obligation to others, most importantly his daughter Daisy, whose "little jointed doll" catches the barber's eye just in time to avert a catastrophic act of retribution. This would be pat sentimentalism, except that the doll hangs on a "gilded spike" above the cashier's desk in a posture that cannot fail to bring to mind the skewered head of another menacing black barber, Melville's Babo in "Benito Cereno." Chesnutt's story overtly disavows retributive violence in favor of prudent restraint, but the calculated allusion to Melville's gory tale of slave insurrection keeps the specter of black violence clearly in view. The colonel escapes unscathed, maintaining that he has proved his theory of black docility, but the narrator adds that "he did not get shaved again in the hotel barber shop" (*Stories*, 412).

"Uncle Wellington's Wives"

While "The Passing of Grandison" and "The Doll" seek to belie Southern attitudes responsible for perpetuating the oppression of blacks, Chesnutt was capable of venting equally stern criticism of the freedman's idealism and pursuit of what he considered a mistaken conception of racial justice. The shiftless protagonist of "Uncle Wellington's Wives," who adopts the more fitting cognomen "Mr. Brayboy" after his Northern exodus, is Chesnutt's most compelling representative of the tendency among newly emancipated African Americans to abandon their cultural foundations in the South to pursue a dream of Northern success.[52] Chesnutt had followed this path with considerable success himself, of course, but he remained harshly critical of idealized African-American expectations of prosperity in Northern cities. Like Tobe, who dreams of unlimited Northern leisure in "Tobe's Tribulations," Uncle Wellington Brayboy is seduced by the image of a "well-formed mulatto" professor from the North, who wears a suit of "dazzling whiteness" and entertains his Southern audience with an account of "the state of ideal equality and happiness enjoyed by colored people at the North" (*Wife*, 204). As a finishing touch to his portrait of a social ideal conceived entirely in terms of whiteness, the professor "assured the excited audience that the intermarriage of the races was common, and that he himself had espoused a white woman" (*Wife*, 205).

Brayboy's romantic adventure in the North ends predictably in disaster when his Irish wife—who, "according to all his preconceived notions, ... ought to have been the acme of uncle Wellington's felicity"—leaves him penniless and alone (*Wife*, 246). His dream of Northern "liberty, equality, privileges" shattered by the realization that social life above the Mason-Dixon line entails "more degrees of inequality than he had ever perceived at the South," Brayboy finally beats his way home to North Carolina, where his wife awaits him in a "whitewashed cabin, shaded with china and mulberry trees" (*Wife*, 250, 260). "De trouble wid Wellin'ton," sermonizes Aunt Milly at the end of the story, "wuz dat he didn' know when he wuz well off. He wuz alluz wishin' fer a change, er studyin' 'bout somethin' new" (*Wife*, 264).

As Myles Raymond Hurd has pointed out, Chesnutt's critique of black emigration in "Uncle Wellington's Wives" enters directly into the famous debate between Booker T. Washington and W. E. B. Du Bois over the proper course of African-American uplift.[53] Hurd explains that the story's consistent assaults on Uncle Wellington's "rose-colored" expectations of Northern equality, coupled with saccharine images of his Southern home, correspond to Washington's positions on emigration and technical education for Southern blacks, to which it might be added that the "well-formed mulatto" professor bears a suggestive resemblance to the erudite Du Bois. It would be a mistake, however, to read "Uncle Wellington's Wives" too narrowly as propaganda for Washington's anti-emigration platform, for Chesnutt makes it clear that another sort of black man—"an active, industrious man" with "the spirit of enterprise and ambition"—might have capitalized on opportunities available to African Americans only in the North (*Wife*, 252). The transition to a new way of life fails in this story not because Chesnutt intends to portray the old plantation, with its deeply inscribed racial arrangements, as a more hospitable setting for postwar blacks than the Northern city. Wellington fails to realize his dream because his "sluggish existence" in the South leaves him susceptible to an incapacitating cultural syndrome the narrator identifies as "inertia" (*Wife*, 252).

In fact, the story makes an illuminating companion to "The Wife of His Youth," for Mr. Ryder—originally "one er de trifflin'es' han's on de plantation"—abandons a woman very much like Aunt Milly on his way to adopting a new way of life and a new personality in the North. Wellington fantasizes about such a transformation, and he actually achieves its symbolic expression by marrying a light-skinned woman, as Ryder ultimately does not. But Wellington, more like Uncle Julius than Mr. Ryder, is dominated by "old habits of life and thought," habits formed under the slave regime, which leave him incapable of profound transformation (*Wife*, 252). The tired old man who retreats to his picturesque Southern cabin at the end of the story is thus anything but an advertisement for Washingtonian reforms.[54] As a study in mental and intellectual inertia, Wellington projects an ominous set of cultural possibilities for Chesnutt, whose art is always directed at altering "old habits of life and thought," especially those that persist in limiting African-American aspirations. Wellington, Chesnutt suggests, is mistaken not for his desire to run from his Southern past, but—like Ryder—for his contemptible ignorance of where, how, and how far to run.

"The Web of Circumstance"

Like so many of Chesnutt's stories, "Uncle Wellington's Wives" registers the psychological toll of a lifetime spent under slavery and peonage. "He was not altogether a bad old man, though very weak and erring," writes the narrator toward the end of the story, implying that Wellington's self-destructive pursuit of an ideal gilded in white is the natural consequence of his skewed imaginative development.

In "The Web of Circumstance," another tale about thwarted postwar aspirations, Chesnutt redirects his moral indignation toward the dominant culture's role in derailing the advancement of talented, industious African Americans.[55] Unlike the "sluggish" and indolent Wellington, Ben Davis is a skillful black artisan whose adherence to a middle-class work ethic has resulted in rapid social and economic improvement. Committed to the belief that "dere ain' nothin' like propputy ter make a pusson feel like a man," he works hard as a blacksmith to pay off his mortgage and warns others against "wastin' yo money on 'scursions to put money in w'ite folks' pockets" (*Wife*, 293). A character filled with "the spirit of enterprise and ambition," as Wellington is not, Ben appears worthy of social recognition by middle-class whites in the story, who share his values of thrift and common sense. "You're talkin' sense, Ben," affirms a white man who overhears his lecture on wasteful habits cultivated under slavery. "Yo'r people will never be respected till they've got property" (*Wife*, 293).

Ben's social and economic advance produces disaster, however, when his alignment with middle-class values and aspirations leads him to covet

Colonel Thornton's rare and expensive whip, an unambiguous symbol of white domination and a reminder of Ben's necessarily ambivalent relation to the concept of "property" in the Southern context. Like the frustrated hero of "Uncle Peter's House," who dreams of owning a large white mansion, "a symbol of power, prosperity, and happiness," Ben attaches great personal significance to the whip (*Stories*, 168). "I wish I had one like it," he exclaims, to which a black bystander responds: " 'Pears ter me Ben gittin' mighty blooded" (*Wife*, 292). Ben argues for his right to own such a token of dominance by again invoking the principles of thrift and industry:

> What's de reason I can't hab a hoss an' buggy an' a whip like Kunnel Tho'nton's, ef I pay fer 'em? ... We colored folks never had no chance ter git nothin' befo' de wah, but ef eve'y nigger in dis town had tuck a keer er his money sence de wah, like I has, an' bought as much lan' as I has, de niggers might 'a' got half de lan' by dis time. (*Wife*, 292–93)

As the logic of this passage implies, Ben's assimilation of a middle-class work ethic presents a tangible threat to white interests. While they applaud his views on property and join Ben in deriding the wasteful habits of his neighbors, whites in the story balk at the realization that black ownership must entail some degree of white subordination. Thus when a black rival steals Colonel Thornton's whip to discredit Ben, the white community galvanizes to condemn the blacksmith as "a negro nihilist, a communist, a secret devotee of Tom Paine and Voltaire, a pupil of the anarchist propaganda, which, if not checked by the stern hand of the law, will fasten its insidious fangs on our social system, and drag it down to ruin" (*Wife*, 298). The outspoken advocate of private property, who has assimilated the dominant culture's work ethic so thoroughly that he covets its symbolic expression, is finally and nonsensically convicted as "a menace to society, for society rests upon the sacred right of property" (*Wife*, 311).

His advance in life abruptly checked by the illogic of a pervasive Southern race consciousness, Ben degenerates into a stolid brute during his five years of hard labor. In a striking anticipation of Dunbar's classic naturalistic novel, *The Sport of the Gods*, he returns to find his family destroyed and determines to exact revenge against Colonel Thornton. In the story's last and most cynical stroke, however, Ben abandons his violent course and is shot down as he flees the colonel's yard, suggesting that while the convict's debasement has limits, his domination by forces beyond his control is absolute.

"Baxter's Procrustes"

The bitter lesson of Ben Davis's rise and fall, a lesson Chesnutt identified with intimately, as his journal attests, is that while the dominant culture demands the spirit of assimilation, the same culture violently rejects any pretense toward social equality for African Americans. As a result, Ben finds himself cut off from the black community, whose values and cultural traditions he has largely abandoned in his pursuit of "propputy," and vilified by the larger society, which sees its "social system" threatened by the advance of this representative of a "barbarian race" (*Wife*, 294). Chesnutt was fascinated—and personally scarred—by the paradox generated by assimilationist gestures on the part of African Americans, a paradox he conveys in *The Marrow of Tradition* by alluding to the mythological figure of Procrustes. "It was a veritable bed of Procrustes, this standard which the whites had set for the negroes," explains the novel's narrator. "Those who grew above it must have their heads cut off, figuratively speaking,—must be forced back to the level assigned to their race; those who fell beneath the standard set had their necks stretched, literally enough, as the ghastly record in the daily papers gave conclusive evidence" (*Marrow*, 260).

The bed of Procrustes is Chesnutt's most comprehensive metaphor for the impossible demands made on postwar African Americans, who were, in his view, as likely to be condemned for their success as for their failure to conform to an incoherent set of social "standards." The Greek bandit who violently stretches or trims his victims until they approximate a uniform type surfaces again in "Baxter's Procrustes," Chesnutt's finest short story, and one of his last. This penetrating satire of the literary community that had failed to embrace Chesnutt on his own terms contains no explicit reference to race, yet behind Baxter's cynical view of contemporary social arrangements and "profound contempt for modern literature" lies a marvelously subtle account of Chesnutt's own dilemma as an African-American author struggling against procrustean forces to gain a hearing in the turn-of-the-century literary marketplace (*Stories*, 415). Jones, the story's laughably pedantic narrator, speculates that the brooding young author of the *Procrustes* harbors some "secret sorrow," which may "arise from a failure" to achieve recognition from an "undiscriminating public" (*Stories*, 415). Chesnutt had reopened his stenography business by the time he wrote "Baxter's Procrustes" in 1903, and, two years after the sour reception of *The Marrow of Tradition*, the book he had hoped would make him famous, he had come to regard his experiment with full-time authorship as a failure. Baxter's wistful conception of social forces that work to limit individual creativity thus tells a deeply personal story about Chesnutt's own frustrated aspirations, and the enigmatic *Procrustes* itself constitutes his parting shot at the race-inflected "standards" used to regulate literary production in the age of Jim Crow.[56]

William Andrews has called "Baxter's Procrustes" the "showcase piece among Chesnutt's short fiction," noting that the story combines the dramatic irony of the dialect tales with some of Chesnutt's most acute descriptive writing in the nondialect mode (Andrews, 132). The story is indeed something of a hybrid literary performance, a trickster narrative in the Uncle Julius tradition with the significant difference that here the trickster remains perfectly silent, his resistance to cultural norms expressed in the act of submitting a blank manuscript as a literary artifact. Jones, whose pompous latinate vocabulary and unwavering materialism betray him as another version of John, provides the bookish frame for Baxter's subversive nonperformance, which functions even more effectively than one of Julius's stories as a "vernacular" rebuke to the superficial values that inform the narrator's perspective. Those values emerge unmistakably in Jones's account of the Bodleian Club, an exclusive literary community whose "*raison d'être*" is the manufacture and collection of rare books. Early in its history, Jones explains, the club

> began the occasional publication of books which should meet the club standard—books in which emphasis should be laid upon the qualities that make a book valuable in the eyes of collectors. Of these, age could not, of course, be imparted, but in the matter of fine and curious bindings, of hand-made linen papers, of uncut or deckle edges, of wide margins and limited editions, the club could control its own publications. (*Stories*, 414)

As if to underscore the superficiality of "the qualities that make a book valuable in the eyes of collectors," Jones adds that "the matter of content was, it must be confessed, a less important consideration." Members of the club had originally insisted that "nothing but the finest products of the human mind should be selected for enshrinement" in its beautiful volumes, but this criterion was soon abandoned in favor of considerations more relevant to what Jones ironically deems "literary values" (*Stories*, 414, 418). When an uncut copy of Bascom's *Essay on Pipes* brings thirty dollars at auction, outpacing essays by Emerson and

Thoreau, club members interpret the sudden inflation of prices as evidence that content has little bearing on market forces that measure the desirability of a literary work. Their relation to the humanistic realm of art defined strictly in material terms, like John's relation to the Southern plantation and its inhabitants, the Bodleians buy and sell books among one another, every member "manifestly interested in keeping up the price" (*Stories*, 415).

At the periphery of this elite society of bibliophiles stands Baxter, "the most scholarly member of the club," who is widely read, according to Jones, but "not so enthusiastic a collector as some of us" (*Stories*, 415). Like Uncle Julius, this subversive prankster conceals his renegade intentions behind a studied deadpan expression, which disguises his contempt for the Bodleian "system" of literary production and valuation (*Stories*, 417). His "philosophy," summarized by Jones, amounts to an elaboration of Chesnutt's procrustean theme: "Society caught every man ... and endeavored to fit him to some preconceived standard.... Life would soon become so monotonously uniform and so uniformly monotonous as to be scarce worth the living" (*Stories*, 416). The Bodleian "system," of course, with its commitment to lavish appearances and contempt for individual content, represents one of the principal homogenizing social tendencies against which Baxter's "gloomy pessimistic philosophy" is directed, but Jones and the other Bodleians confidently interpret his pessimism as an endorsement of their own values and priorities (*Stories*, 415). After an exhaustive analysis of the volume's "intricate blind-tooling" and "rubricated initials," Jones declares—more profoundly than he realizes—that Baxter's *Procrustes* "might be said to represent all that the Bodleian [stands] for," and that the volume is "in itself sufficient to justify the club's existence" (*Stories*, 420).

Jones's language here echoes a maneuver familiar to readers of the dialect tales, in which John frequently succeeds in coopting the voice of resistance, offering his own interpretations of Uncle Julius's stories as normative.[57] Julius's susceptibility to this sort of coercion, whether John emerges as a reliable interpreter or not, constituted a serious annoyance to Chesnutt, who balked at Julius's ambivalent relation to such plantation tradition icons as Uncle Remus. Like John, the Northern capitalist to whom Julius's stories are nothing but a form of postwar currency, Jones and the Bodleians seek to incorporate Baxter's procrustean philosophy into their own system of material values. Members of the club thus praise Baxter's "dissatisfaction with an unjustified optimism," his "serious view of life as a thing to be endured as patiently as might be," his insight into "the shams by which the optimist sought to delude himself into the view that life was a desirable thing" (*Stories*, 419–20). Eager to praise but unwilling to engage Baxter's "serious view of life," Jones redirects the author's critique by noting that the black-letter type on the *Procrustes* signifies "a philosophic pessimism enlightened by the conviction that in duty one might find, after all, an excuse for life and a hope for humanity" (*Stories*, 420).

If the *Procrustes* contained even a line of blank verse, as it purports to, this dexterous effort to convert Baxter's mockery of Bodleian values into a celebration of the club's principles might succeed, much as John's interpretive gestures often succeed in muting the force of Julius's vernacular resistance. But the book is a pure blank, its uninterrupted margins conveying a more penetrating statement about society's procrustean influence than Baxter's misanthropic poetry ever could. Like Viney in "The Dumb Witness" or Tom Taylor in "The Doll," Baxter employs a devastating silence to articulate a critique that is impervious to distortion, a critique that exposes the Bodleian system as grounded in "sham optimism" and crass materialism. In providing members of the club with exactly the form of cultural expression they covet—an ornamental literary artifact without content—Baxter conveys his philosophic rage at social and aesthetic "standards" that restrict individuality, demonstrating that such standards amount to an insidious form of censorship and result in the demise of a substantive cultural life.

Initially disgusted by Baxter's duplicity, most of the members discard their uncut copies of the *Procrustes*, dismissing the book as a mean-spirited affront to their aesthetic values, but it gradually dawns on several of the more thoughtful Bodleians that the *Procrustes* constitutes "a work of art" that is "entirely logical" "from the collector's point of view" (*Stories*, 421–22). "The true collector," comments the club's president, "loves wide margins, and the *Procrustes*, being all margin, merely touches the vanishing point of the perspective" (*Stories*, 422). The story thus complicates the didactic force of Baxter's hoax—don't judge a book by its cover—by affirming the ominous power of the dominant culture to ignore even the starkest forms of critique. The tale ends by demonstrating the resilience of a cultural disposition committed to illusion and motivated by self-interest, a disposition capable of worshiping books while ignoring, in Robert Hemenway's words, "the human truths they contain" (Hemenway, 1974, 178).

Chesnutt continued to write and publish occasional stories after 1904, when "Baxter's Procrustes" appeared in the *Atlantic Monthly*, but the sense of possibility with which he had embarked on his professional writing career had clearly yielded to a sense of futility. In his 1880 journal, he had declared his intention to spark a "moral revolution" that would remove "the unjust spirit of caste which is so insidious as to pervade a whole nation, and so powerful as to subject a whole race and all connected with it to scorn and social ostracism" (*Journals,* 139). "It is the province of literature," he had insisted, "to open the way." This belief in the revolutionary capacity of literature pervades Chesnutt's early stories, like "The Sheriff's Children" (1889), and his confidence in the possibility of genuine moral transformation was apparently still running high at the end of the century, as the uplifting conclusion to *The Marrow of Tradition* (1901) suggests. The philosophic pessimism of "Baxter's Procrustes," however, sounds a very different note, one that Chesnutt would sustain in his 1905 novel, *The Colonel's Dream,* another account of socially progressive ambitions shattered by intransigent racial prejudice. By late 1905, when he formally abandoned his dream of a professional writing career, Chesnutt had come to regard the "high, holy purpose" that had fueled his literary ambitions with a measure of Baxterian irony and bemused detachment. He continued to work vigorously for African-American rights, remaining vocal in the struggle against racial oppression until his death in 1932, but the youthful confidence that literature might effect a moral revolution had disappeared behind Baxter's inscrutable smile.

Notes to Part One

1. *The Journals of Charles W. Chesnutt,* ed. Richard H. Brodhead (Durham, N.C.: Duke Univ. Press, 1993), 154. Hereafter cited in text as *Journals.*

2. The earliest version of "Rena Walden" is a 51-page typescript held in the Chesnutt Collection at Fisk University Library. See William Andrews's excellent discussion of the story's evolution between 1889 and 1900 in *The Literary Career of Charles W. Chesnutt* (Baton Rouge: Louisiana State Univ. Press, 1980). Hereafter cited in text.

3. Chesnutt's correspondence with Gilder is quoted selectively in Helen M. Chesnutt's *Charles Waddell Chesnutt: Pioneer of the Color Line* (Chapel Hill: Univ. of North Carolina Press, 1952), 56–59. Hereafter cited in text.

4. A good deal of critical literature centers on Chesnutt's complicated relationship to the plantation tradition. Two essays that offer particularly compelling insight into the deconstructive energies at work in his stories are Robert C. Nowatzki, " 'Passing' in a White Genre: Charles W. Chesnutt's Negotiation of the Plantation Tradition," *American Literary Realism* 27 (Fall 1995): 20–36;

and Craig Werner, "The Framing of Charles W. Chesnutt: Practical Deconstruction in the Afro American Tradition," in *Southern Literature and Literary Theory,* ed. Jefferson Humphries (Athens: Univ. of Georgia Press, 1990), 339–65.

5. Chesnutt had already unsuccessfully approached the firm about a collection of stories in 1891.

6. J. Noel Heermance provides a useful discussion of Chesnutt's decision to withhold information about his racial identity in *Charles W. Chesnutt: America's First Great Black Novelist* (Hamden, Conn.: Archon Books, 1974), 69.

7. Richard H. Brodhead has written extensively on Chesnutt's unique relation to the publishing establishment of his era. See especially his *Cultures of Letters: Scenes of Reading and Writing in Nineteenth-Century America* (Chicago: Univ. of Chicago Press, 1993).

8. Charles Waddell Chesnutt, *The Conjure Woman and Other Conjure Tales,* ed. Richard H. Brodhead (Durham, N.C.: Duke Univ. Press, 1993), 34. For its insightful introduction and judicious inclusion of the seven dialect stories omitted from *The Conjure Woman,* this superb edition deserves to be the standard text for Chesnutt's Uncle Julius tales. Hereafter cited in text as *Conjure.*

9. Robert Hemenway, "The Functions of Folklore in Charles Chesnutt's *The Conjure Woman,*" *Journal of the Folklore Institute* 13 (1976): 289.

10. Ben Slote expands on the role of minstrelsy in "The Goophered Grapevine" in a fascinating essay, "Listening to 'The Goophered Grapevine' and Hearing Raisins Sing," *American Literary History* 6 (Winter 1994): 684–94, reproduced in part 3 of this volume. Hereafter cited in text.

11. In "Dave's Neckliss," an Uncle Julius tale that was not included in the original *Conjure Woman* collection, John explains that Julius's stories expose "the simple but intensely human inner life of slavery" (*Conjure,* 124).

12. Eric J. Sundquist, *To Wake the Nations: Race in the Making of American Literature* (Cambridge: Harvard Univ. Press, 1993), 362. Hereafter cited in text.

13. Ralph Ellison, "Richard Wright's Blues," in *Shadow and Act* (New York: Random House, 1964), 90. Richard E. Baldwin make a point of comparing Ellison's conception of the blues to Chesnutt's art of conjure in "The Art of *The Conjure Woman,*" *American Literature* 43 (1971): 392. The most ambitious attempt to conceptualize the blues as a paradigm for African-American cultural expression is Houston A. Baker's *Blues, Ideology, and Afro-American Literature* (Chicago: Univ. of Chicago Press, 1984), a book that, for all its stunning insight, fails to notice Chesnutt's remarkable contribution to an emergent blues aesthetic at the end of the nineteenth century. Baker's compelling thoughts on Chesnutt's dialect fiction make their way into a later and equally groundbreaking work, *Modernism and the Harlem Renaissance* (Chicago: Univ. of Chicago Press, 1987), 41–47, reprinted in part 3 of this volume.

14. Eric Selinger discusses the significance of Chesnutt's pun in "Aunts, Uncles, Audience: Gender and Genre in Charles Chesnutt's *The Conjure Woman,*" *Black American Literature Forum* 25 (Winter 1991): 673. Hereafter cited in text.

15. John F. Callahan describes the dual audience structure of Chesnutt's "Po' Sandy" in *In the African-American Grain: The Pursuit of Voice in Twentieth-Century Black Fiction* (Urbana: Univ. of Illinois Press, 1988).

16. Robert Stepto makes a very different point about John's sensibility in " 'The Simple but Intensely Human Inner Life of Slavery': Storytelling and the Revision of History in Charles W. Chesnutt's 'Uncle Julius Stories,' " in *History and Tradition in Afro-American Culture,* ed. Gunter H. Lenz (Frankfurt: Campus, 1984), 22–55. Stepto argues persuasively—though, for me, inconclusively—that John gradually acquires a more enlightened understanding of African-American culture through his exposure to Julius's stories.

17. "Mars Jeems's Nightmare" appeared originally in *The Conjure Woman* in 1899.

18. The term "New Negro" is usually associated with Alain Locke's landmark 1925 anthology of Harlem Renaissance writings, *The New Negro* (rpt. New York: Atheneum, 1974), yet Wilson Moses has shown that the term was already widely in use by the late 1880s. See his essay, "The Lost World of the New Negro, 1895–1919: Black Literary and Intellectual Life before the 'Renaissance,' " *Black American Literature Forum* 21 (Spring 1987): 71–72. Eric Sundquist connects Chesnutt's story with the "New Negro" conception in *To Wake the Nations,* pp. 333–36.

19. It is useful to remember that "Mars Jeems's Nightmare" is a late conjure story, probably written in 1898, nearly 10 years after Chesnutt had made the premature decision to drop Uncle Julius as a mouthpiece. The tale's apparent focus on the cultural predicament of Julius's grandchildren might therefore be taken as a measure of Chesnutt's desire to write a different sort of conjure story than either "The Goophered Grapevine" or "Po' Sandy," one that addresses—despite its recreation of the plantation setting—issues relevant to contemporary African-American life.

20. "The Sheriff's Children," New York *Independent,* Nov. 7, 1889, reprinted in *The Wife of His Youth and Other Stories of the Color Line* (1899; rpt. Ann Arbor: Univ. of Michigan Press, 1968), 90. Herafter cited in text as *Wife.*

21. Chesnutt, *The Marrow of Tradition* (Boston: Houghton Mifflin, 1901), reprinted in *The African-American Novel in the Age of Reaction: Three Classics,* ed. William Andrews (New York: Penguin, 1992), 284. Hereafter cited in text as *Marrow.* In its ambiguous juxtaposition of these highly charged stereotypes—the docile slave and the masterful "Angry-Saxon"—"Mars Jeems's Nightmare" anticipates one of Chesnutt's most interesting and enigmatic nondialect stories, "The Doll."

22. "The Conjurer's Revenge" was first published in *The Overland Monthly* 13 (1889): 623–29.

23. Selinger examines the gender dynamics of conjure as performed by male and female practitioners (665–88).

24. "Sis' Becky's Pickaninny" appeared originally in *The Conjure Woman* in 1899.

25. Given John's therapeutic assumptions, it may seem odd that in addition to "letters from the North" he invites the hands to serenade Annie with plantation songs. This anomaly might be explained by the fact that, by the late nineteenth century, touring groups had introduced Northern audiences to highly stylized versions of African-American musical spiritualism. Ironically, exposure to such a mediated form of African-American folk expression might therefore be considered entirely consistent with John's desire to avoid "infection" by Southern influences.

26. Julius's statement about the value of the rabbit's foot would seem to encourage the idea that conjure resists the potentially exploitative conditions of an exchange economy. Yet it is important to remember that Aunt Peggy's services often possess a specific cash value (Mars Dugal' pays her $10 in "The Goophered Grapevine"), and that the spiritual power of conjure is frequently available to the highest bidder, black or white.

27. Melvin Dixon, "The Teller as Folk Trickster in Chesnutt's *The Conjure Woman,*" *CLA Journal* 18 (1974): 159.

28. "The Gray Wolf's Ha'nt" originally appeared in *The Conjure Woman* in 1899.

29. Selinger speculates that the passage John is reading might logically conclude this way: "It presents to our intelligence an appearance of multiplicity: a variety of histories or processes in which transformation occurs. Thus, while complete and deductive interpretation may be almost hopeless, partial and inductive interpretations, rendered in the mode of narrative under the auspices of the imagination, are certainly possible" (679). Dixon draws a similar conclusion when he describes John's philosophy as less inept than "massively inapt" (57).

30. Nowatzki provides an interesting account of the way John's philosophical reading positions Julius's vernacular performance (26).

31. "Hot-Foot Hannibal" appeared originally in the *Atlantic Monthly* 83 (January 1899): 49–56.

32. Cable's letter to Chesnutt is cited in Andrews (25).

33. See, for example, Michael G. Cooke, *Afro-American Literature in the Twentieth Century: The Achievement of Intimacy* (New Haven: Yale Univ. Press, 1984), 58–59; and Eugene Terry, "The Shadow of Slavery in Charles Chesnutt's *The Conjure Woman,*" *Ethnic Groups* 4 (1982): 124.

34. Selinger maintains that the "return of stock figures and sentimentality in 'Hot-Foot Hannibal' suggests that Chesnutt has reached some generic boundary, and is in retreat" (683).

35. Written in 1897, "The Dumb Witness" survives in several manuscript versions in the Charles Waddell Chesnutt Papers at Fisk University. A revised

and adapted version of the story appears in Chesnutt's 1905 novel, *The Colonel's Dream*, and a version based on the original manuscript has been published by Richard Brodhead in *The Conjure Woman and Other Conjure Tales*.

36. "Dave's Neckliss" appeared originally in the October 1889 *Atlantic Monthly*. Despite its obvious power, the story was not included in Houghton Mifflin's collection of Chesnutt's Uncle Julius tales, ostensibly because it lacks the element of conjure. Some critics, including Richard Brodhead, have speculated that the tale was overlooked because of its graphic indictment of slavery. See Brodhead's introduction to *The Conjure Woman and Other Conjure Tales*, pp. 17–19.

37. Indeed, "Dave's Neckliss" bears more in common with Franz Kafka's nightmarish "The Metamorphosis" than with Joel Chandler Harris's Uncle Remus tales, as Frances Richardson Keller has observed in *An American Crusade: The Life of Charles Waddell Chesnutt* (Provo: Brigham Young Univ. Press, 1978), 141. Chesnutt's late story "Concerning Father" also bears a striking, if coincidental, resemblance to Kafka's "The Judgment."

38. "A Victim of Heredity; or, Why the Darkey Loves Chicken" was first published in *Self-Culture Magazine* 11 (July 1900): 404–9.

39. Houston Baker discusses a dynamic interplay between "the form of mastery" and the "mastery of form" in Washington's representation of the chicken thief in *Up from Slavery*. See *Modernism and the Harlem Renaissance*, pp. 33–36.

40. An interesting companion to "Tobe's Tribulations," in which Tobe sleeps away his freedom, is the story "A Deep Sleeper," in which Skundus and his postwar counterpart, Tom, use sleep as a cover for subversive behavior. Both stories appear in Brodhead's *The Conjure Woman and Other Conjure Tales*. "Tobe's Tribulations" first appeared in *Southern Workman* 29 (November 1900): 656–64.

41. Dunbar's novel *The Sport of the Gods* describes a black family's unsuccessful emigration to New York and subsequent return to the postwar Southern plantation.

42. Sundquist maintains that the point of the story "is to make the reader hear Tobe's voice—hear the voice of failed emancipation as well as the surviving voice of Africans in America, scarred so deeply by the experience of slavery and expressed from the 'bottom' of life" (317).

43. "Lonesome Ben" appeared in *Southern Workman* 29 (March 1900): 137–45.

44. Quoted in Andrews (5).

45. William Andrews, introduction to *The Collected Stories of Charles W. Chesnutt* (New York: Mentor, 1992), xiv.

46. Werner Sollers explains that "Liza Jane, who is South and slavery, black culture and black consciousness, folk and past, mother culture and memory, or, in one word, the world of *descent*, represents everything that the Blue

Veins have been trying so hard to eradicate and to build boundaries against. She is defined by contrast and identified by negation." See *Beyond Ethnicity: Consent and Descent in American Culture* (New York: Oxford Univ. Press, 1986), 161.

47. "The Sheriff's Children" first appeared in the New York *Independent* on November 7, 1889.

48. "Her Virginia Mammy" was first published in *The Wife of His Youth* in 1899.

49. Sundquist points out that Mrs. Harper's restraint is conveyed in the text with dashes, which Sundquist deems "the sign of passing, the orthographic representation of secrecy written into textuality" (401).

50. "The Passing of Grandison" first appeared in *The Wife of His Youth* in 1899.

51. "The Doll" first appeared in *Crisis* 3 (1912): 248–52; the story is reprinted in Sylvia Lyons Render's indispensable collection *The Short Fiction of Charles W. Chesnutt*, ed. Sylvia Lyons Render (Washington, D.C.: Howard Univ. Press, 1974), 405–412. Hereafter cited in text as *Stories*.

52. "Uncle Wellington's Wives" was first published in *The Wife of His Youth* in 1899.

53. Myles Raymond Hurd, "Booker T., Blacks, and Brogues: Chesnutt's Sociohistorical Links to Realism in 'Uncle Wellington's Wives,' " *American Literary Realism* 26 (Winter 1994): 19–29.

54. Arlene Elder offers insight into Chesnutt's stand in the ongoing argument between Washington and Du Bois in "Chesnutt on Washington: An Essential Ambivalence," *Phylon* 38 (1977): 186–97.

55. "The Web of Circumstance" originally appeared in *The Wife of His Youth* in 1899.

56. As biographers have long stressed, "Baxter's Procrustes" constitutes Chesnutt's bid for psychic retribution after his abortive attempt to join Cleveland's exclusive Rowfant Club in 1902. Rejected for membership because, as Helen Chesnutt puts it, "the time hadn't come" for the inclusion of an African-American writer, Chesnutt must have taken great pleasure in exposing the club's hypocritical commitment to humanistic values (Helen Chesnutt, 244). To compound the irony of Baxter's ploy, it is interesting to note that members of the Rowfant Club purchased most of the copies of a special pretrade edition of *The Conjure Woman* in 1899, making that collection an even more explicit model for the subversive tactics of the *Procrustes*. To compound the irony again, "Baxter's Procrustes" was itself reissued in a limited edition by the Rowfant Club in 1966. See Robert Hemenway, " 'Baxter's Procrustes': Irony and Protest," *CLA Journal* 18 (1974): 173. Hereafter cited in text.

57. Consider, for example, the many ways in which Julius's stories, for all their subversive power, tend to reinforce rather than dislodge John's condescending view of African-American culture. Contrary to Robert Stepto's intrigu-

ing contention that John develops sympathy for Julius over time, there is little compelling evidence that the old man's tales do anything but strengthen John's sense of racial mastery (Stepto, 33). For a brilliant discussion of this issue as it affects the teaching of Chesnutt's stories in the contemporary classroom, see Ben Slote's "Listening to 'The Goophered Grapevine' and Hearing Raisins Sing."

Part 2

THE WRITER

Introduction

While Chesnutt's literary career was relatively brief, the vast majority of his short fiction having been written in the two decades between 1885 and 1905, he remained an active commentator on social and literary issues until nearly the end of his life in 1932. In making selections from his nonfiction prose, I have therefore sought to offer a variety of writings from different periods of Chesnutt's life, beginning with two 1880 journal entries in which the ambitious young Southerner announces his literary aspirations, and ending with the famous retrospective essay "Post-Bellum—Pre-Harlem," published in 1931. In between are three important statements dealing with issues that occupied Chesnutt throughout his life.

The editorial "What Is a White Man?," which appeared in the New York *Independent* on May 30, 1889, confronts the byzantine logic of racial classification in American law and society, a topic Chesnutt would return to constantly in stories of the color line. In "The Future American," a series of three essays printed in the Boston *Evening Transcript* in 1900, one of which is reproduced here, he discusses the controversial subject of racial "amalgamation," predicting that an inevitable mingling of the races will put an end to "the dream of a pure white race, of the Anglo-Saxon type, for the United States." Readers may be surprised by Chesnutt's confidence that racial prejudice in America "is more apparent than real," and by his firm belief that the vestiges of race consciousness will be eliminated as a natural result of racial blending. More surprising still, perhaps, is Chesnutt's attitude toward African-American folk culture in "Superstitions and Folklore of the South," a 1901 essay on the disappearing traditions of conjure and voodoo—"relics of ancestral barbarism"—in the American South. Sounding considerably more like the Ohioan John than like Uncle Julius, Chesnutt notes with seeming enthusiasm that education is the key to dispelling "the absurdities of superstition" that persist in benighting poor black Southerners. Readers may be intrigued by Eric Sundquist's contention (in part 3) that Chesnutt—like Julius—is toying with readers who may be too eager to concur with this condescending view of African-American culture, but this reading of the essay is by no means conclusive.

Part 2 ends with Chesnutt's effort to situate his literary achievement in the context of American cultural life at the turn of the century, a project he effectively summarizes in the essay's title, "Post-Bellum—Pre-Harlem." With characteristic deference, he discusses his relationship to contemporaries like Joel Chandler Harris, Thomas Dixon, Thomas Nelson Page, and others, as well as his view of the art and literature of the emerging Harlem Renaissance. His sense of his own career as a bridge between two vastly different epochs in African-American cultural life is too modest, for it obscures Chesnutt's distinctive achievement, but this self-analysis offers one important way to measure his significance as a writer.

Journal Entry: March 16, 1880

Judge Tourgée has sold the "Fool's Errand," I understand, for $20,000. I suppose he has already received a large royalty on the sale of the first few editions. The work has gained an astonishing degree of popularity, and is to be translated into French.

Now, Judge Tourgée's book is about the South,—the manners, customs, modes of thought, etc. which are prevalent in this section of the country. Judge Tourgée is a Northern man, who has lived at the South since the war, until recently. He knows a great deal about the politics, history, and laws of the South. He is a close observer of men and things, and has exercised this faculty of observation upon the character of the Southern people. Nearly all his stories are more or less about colored people, and this very feature is one source of their popularity. There is something romantic, to the Northern mind, about the Southern negro, as commonplace and vulgar as he seems to us who come in contact with him every day. And there is a romantic side to the history of these people. Men are always more ready to extend their sympathy to those at a distance, than to the suffering ones in their midst. And the North, their eyes not blinded by the dirt and the hazy moral and social atmosphere which surrounds the average negro in the South, their interest not blunted by familiarity with the state of affairs in the South, or prejudiced by a love of "our institutions"—sees the South as it is; or is ever eager for something that will show it in a correct light. They see in the Colored people a race, but recently emancipated from a cruel bondage; struggling for education, for a higher social and moral life, against wealth, intelligence, and race prejudice, which are all united to keep them down. And they hear the cry of the oppressed and struggling ones, and extend a hand to help them; they lend a willing ear to all that is spoken or written concerning their character, habits, etc. And if Judge Tourgée, with his necessarily limited intercourse with colored people,

From *The Journals of Charles W. Chesnutt*, ed. Richard H. Brodhead (Durham, N.C.: Duke Univ. Press, 1993), 124–26, 139–40.

and with his limited stay in the South, can write such interesting descriptions, such vivid pictures of Southern life and character as to make himself rich and famous, why could not a colored man, who has lived among colored people all his life; who is familiar with their habits, their ruling passions, their prejudices; their whole moral and social condition; their public and private ambitions; their religious tendencies and habits;—why could not a colored man who knew all this, and who, besides, had possessed such opportunities for observation and conversation with the better class of white men in the South as to understand their modes of thinking; who was familiar with the political history of the country, and especially with all the phases of the slavery question;— why could not such a man, if he possessed the same ability, write a far better book about the South than Judge Tourgée or Mrs. Stowe has written? Answer who can! But the man is yet to make his appearance; and if I can't be the man I shall be the first to rejoice at his *début* and give God speed! to his work.

I intend to record my impressions of men and things, and such incidents or conversations which take place within my knowledge, with a view to future use in literary work. I shall not record stale negro minstrel jokes, or worn out newspaper squibs on the "man and brother." I shall leave the realm of fiction, where most of this stuff is manufactured, and come down to hard facts. There are many things about the colored people which are peculiar, to some extent, to them, and which are interesting to any thoughtful observer, and would be doubly interesting to people who know little about them.

Journal Entry: May 29, 1880

I think I must write a book. I am almost afraid to undertake a book so early and with so little experience in composition. But it has been my cherished dream, and I feel an influence that I cannot resist calling me to the task. Besides, I do not know but I am as well prepared as some other successful writers. A fair knowledge of the classics, a speaking acquaintance with the modern languages, an intimate friendship with literature, etc.; seven years experience in the school room, two years of married life, and a habit of studying character have I think, left me not entirely unprepared to write even a book. Fifteen years of life in the South, in one of the most eventful eras of its history; among a people whose life is rich in the elements of romance; under conditions calculated to stir one's soul to the very depths;—I think there is here a fund of experience, a supply of material, which a skillful person could work up with tremendous effect. Besides, if I do write, I shall write for a purpose, a high, holy purpose, and this will inspire me to greater effort. The object of my writings would be not so much the elevation of the colored people as the elevation of the whites,—for I consider the unjust spirit of caste which is so insidious as to pervade a whole nation, and so powerful as to subject a whole race and all connected with it to scorn and social ostracism—I consider this a barrier to the moral progress of the American people; and I would be one of the first to head a determined, organized crusade against it. Not a fierce indiscriminate onslaught; not an appeal to force, for this is something that force can but slightly affect; but a moral revolution which must be brought about in a different manner. The Abolitionists stirred up public opinion on behalf of the slave, by appealing in trumpet tones to those principles of justice and humanity which were only lying dormant in the Northern heart. The iron hand of power set the slave free from personal bondage, and by admitting him to all the rights of citizenship—the ballot, education—is fast freeing him from the greater bondage of ignorance. But the subtle almost indefinable feeling of repulsion toward the negro, which is common to most Americans—and easily enough accounted for—, cannot be stormed and taken by assault; the garrison will not capitulate; so their position must be mined, and we will find ourselves in their midst before they think it.

This work is of a twofold character. The negro's part is to prepare himself for social recognition and equality; and it is the province of literature to open the way for him to get it—to accustom the public mind to the idea; and while amusing them to lead them on imperceptibly, unconsciously step by step to the desired state of feeling. If I can do anything to further this work, and can see any likelihood of obtaining success in it, I would gladly devote my life to the work.

What Is a White Man?

The fiat having gone forth from the wise men of the South that the "all-pervading, all-conquering Anglo-Saxon race" must continue forever to exercise exclusive control and direction of the government of this so-called Republic, it becomes important to every citizen who values his birthright to know who are included in this grandiloquent term. It is of course perfectly obvious that the writer or speaker who used this expression—perhaps Mr. Grady of Georgia—did not say what he meant. It is not probable that he meant to exclude from full citizenship the Celts and Teutons and Gauls and Slavs who make up so large a proportion of our population; he hardly meant to exclude the Jews, for even the most ardent fire-eater would hardly venture to advocate the disfranchisement of the thrifty race whose mortgages cover so large a portion of Southern soil. What the eloquent gentleman really meant by his high-sounding phrase was simply the white race; and the substance of the argument of that school of Southern writers to which he belongs, is simply that for the good of the country the Negro should have no voice in directing the government or public policy of the Southern States or of the nation.

But it is evident that where the intermingling of the races has made such progress as it has in this country, the line which separates the races must in many instances have been practically obliterated. And there has arisen in the United States a very large class of the population who are certainly not Negroes in an ethnological sense, and whose children will be no nearer Negroes than themselves. In view, therefore, of the very positive ground taken by the white leaders of the South, where most of these people reside, it becomes in the highest degree important to them to know what race they belong to. It ought to be also a matter of serious concern to the Southern white people; for if their zeal for good government is so great that they contemplate the practical overthrow of the Constitution and laws of the United States to secure it, they ought

From the New York *Independent*, May 30, 1889, pp. 693–94.

at least to be sure that no man entitled to it by their own argument, is robbed of a right so precious as that of free citizenship; the "all-pervading, all-conquering Anglo-Saxon race" ought to set as high a value on American citizenship as the all-conquering Roman placed upon the franchise of his State two thousand years ago. This discussion would of course be of little interest to the genuine Negro, who is entirely outside of the charmed circle, and must content himself with the acquisition of wealth, the pursuit of learning and other such privileges as his "best friends" may find it consistent with the welfare of the nation to allow him; but to every other good citizen the inquiry ought to be a momentous one, What is a white man?

In spite of the virulence and universality of race prejudice in the United States, the human intellect long ago revolted at the manifest absurdity of classifying men fifteen-sixteenths white as black men; and hence there grew up a number of laws in different states of the Union defining the limit which separated the white and colored races, which was, when these laws took their rise and is now to a large extent, the line which separates freedom and opportunity from slavery or hopeless degradation. Some of these laws are of legislative origin; others are judge-made laws, brought out by the exigencies of special cases which came before the courts for determination. Some day they will, perhaps, become mere curiosities of jurisprudence; the "black laws" will be bracketed with the "blue laws," and will be at best but landmarks by which to measure the progress of the nation. But today these laws are in active operation, and they are, therefore, worthy of attention; for every good citizen ought to know the law, and, if possible, to respect it; and if not worthy of respect, it should be changed by the authority which enacted it....

The states vary slightly in regards to what constitutes a mulatto or person of color, and as to what proportion of white blood should be sufficient to remove the disability of color. As a general rule, less than one-fourth of Negro blood left the individual white—in theory; race questions being, however, regulated very differently in practice. In Missouri, by the code of 1855, still in operation, so far as not inconsistent with the Federal Constitution and laws, "any person other than a Negro, any one of whose grandmothers or grandfathers is or shall have been a Negro, tho all of his or her progenitors except those descended from the Negro may have been white persons, shall be deemed a mulatto." Thus the color-line is drawn at one-fourth of Negro blood, and persons with only one-eighth are white....

Under the *code noir* of Louisiana, the descendant of a white and a quadroon is white, thus drawing the line at one-eighth of Negro blood.... In Ohio the rule, as established by numerous decisions of the Supreme Court, was that a preponderance of white blood constituted a person as a white man in the eye of the law, and entitled him to the exercise of all the civil rights of a white man. By a retrogressive step the color-line was extended in 1861 in the case of marriage, which by statute was forbidden between a person of pure white blood and one having a visible admixture of African blood....

But it is Georgia, the *alma genetrix* of the chain gang, which merits the questionable distinction of having the harshest set of color laws. By the law of Georgia the term "person of color" is defined to mean "all such as have an admixture of Negro blood, and the term 'Negro' includes mulattoes." This definition is perhaps restricted somewhat by another provision, by which "all Negroes, mestizoes, and their descendants, having one-eighth of Negro or mulatto blood in their veins, shall be known in this state as persons of color.".... It is further provided that "the marriage relation between white persons and persons of African descent is forever prohibited, and such marriages shall be null and void." This is a very sweeping provision; it will be noticed that the term "persons of color," previously defined, is not employed, the expression "persons of African descent" being used instead. A court which was so inclined would find no difficulty in extending this provision of the law to the remotest strain of African blood. The marriage relation is forever prohibited. Forever is a long time. There is a colored woman in Georgia said to be worth $300,000—an immense fortune in the poverty stricken South. With a few hundred such women in that state, possessing a fair degree of good looks, the color line would shrivel up like a scroll in the heat of competition for their hands in marriage....

Whatever the wisdom or justice of these laws, there is one objection to them which is not given sufficient prominence in the consideration of the subject, even where it is discussed at all; they make mixed blood a *prima-facie* proof of illegitimacy. It is a fact that at present, in the United States, a colored man or woman whose complexion is white or nearly white is presumed, in the absence of any knowledge of his or her antecedents, to be the offspring of a union not sanctioned by law. And by a curious but not uncommon process, such persons are not held in the same low estimation as white people in the same position. The sins of their fathers are not visited upon the children, in that regard at least; and their mothers' lapses from virtue are regarded either as misfortunes or as faults excusable under the circumstances. But in spite of all this, illegitimacy is not a desirable distinction, and is likely to become less so as these people of mixed blood advance in wealth and social standing. This presumption of illegitimacy was once, perhaps, true of the majority of such persons; but the times have changed. More than half of the colored people of the United States are of mixed blood; they marry and are given in marriage, and they beget children of complexions similar to their own. Whether or not, therefore, laws which stamp these children as illegitimate, and which by indirection establish a lower standard of morality for a large part of the population than the remaining part is judged by, are wise laws; and whether or not the purity of the white race could not be as well preserved by the exercise of virtue, and the operation of those natural laws which are so often quoted by Southern writers as the justification for all sorts of Southern "policies"—are questions which the good citizen may at least turn over in his mind occasionally, pending the settlement of other complications which have grown out of the presence of the Negro on this continent.

The Future American:
What the Race Is Likely to Become
in the Process of Time

The future American race is a popular theme for essayists, and has been much discussed. Most expressions upon the subject, however, have been characterized by a conscious or unconscious evasion of some of the main elements of the problem involved in the formation of a future American race, or, to put it perhaps more correctly, a future ethnic type that shall inhabit the northern part of the western continent....

The popular theory is that the future American race will consist of a harmonious fusion of the various European elements which now make up our heterogeneous population. The result is to be something infinitely superior to the best component elements. This perfection of type—for no good American could for a moment doubt that it will be as perfect as everything else American—is to be brought about by a combination of all the best characteristics of the different European races, and the elimination, by some strange alchemy, of all their undesirable traits—for even a good American will admit that European races, now and then, have some undesirable traits when they first come over. It is a beautiful, a hopeful, and to the eye of faith, a thrilling prospect. The defect of the argument, however, lies in the incompleteness of the premises, and its obliviousness to certain facts of human nature and human history.

Before putting forward any theory upon the subject, it may well be enough to remark that recent scientific research has swept away many hoary anthropological fallacies. It has been demonstrated that the shape or size of the head has little or nothing to do with the civilization or average intelligence of a race; that language, so recently lauded as an infallible test of racial origin, is of absolutely no value in this connection, its distribution being dependent upon other conditions than race. Even

From the Boston *Evening Transcript*, August 18, 1900, p. 20

color, upon which the social structure of the United States is so largely based, has been proved no test of race. The conception of a pure Aryan, Indo-European race has been abandoned in scientific circles, and the secret of the progress of Europe has been found in racial heterogeneity, rather than in racial purity.... By modern research, the unity of the human race has been proved (if it needed any proof to the careful or fair-minded observer), and the differentiation of races by selection and environment has been so stated as to be proved itself. Greater emphasis has been placed upon environment as a factor in ethnic development, and what has been called "the vulgar theory of race," as accounting for progress and culture, has been relegated to the limbo of exploded dogmas....

Proceeding then upon the firm basis laid down by science and the historical parallel, it ought to be quite clear that the future American race—the future American ethnic type—will be formed of a mingling, in a yet to be ascertained proportion, of the various racial varieties which make up the present population of the United States; or, to extend the area a little farther, of the various peoples of the northern hemisphere of the western continent; for, if certain recent tendencies are an index of the future, it is not safe to fix the boundaries of the future United States anywhere short of the Arctic Ocean on the north and the Isthmus of Panama on the south....

By the eleventh census, the ratios of which will probably not be changed materially by the census now under way, the total population of the United States was about 65,000,000, of which about seven million were black and colored, and something over 200,000 were of Indian blood. It is then in the three broad types—white, black, and Indian— that the future American race will find the material for its formation. Any dream of a pure white race, of the Anglo-Saxon type, for the United States, may as well be abandoned as impossible, even if desirable. That such a future race will be predominantly white may well be granted— unless climate in the course of time should modify existing types; that it will call itself white is reasonably sure; that it will conform closely to the white type is likely; but that it will have absorbed and assimilated the blood of the other two races mentioned is as certain as the operation of any law well can be that deals with so uncertain a quantity as the human race.

Superstitions and Folklore of the South

During a recent visit to North Carolina, after a long absence, I took occasion to inquire into the latter-day prevalence of the old-time belief in what was known as "conjuration" or "goopher," my childish recollection of which I have elsewhere embodied into a number of stories. The derivation of the word "goopher" I do not know, nor whether any other writer than myself has recognized its existence, though it is in frequent use in certain parts of the South. The origin of this curious superstition itself is perhaps more easily traceable. It probably grew, in the first place, out of African fetichism, which was brought over from the dark continent along with the dark people. Certain features, too, suggest a distant affinity with Voodooism, or snake worship, a cult which seems to have been indigenous to tropical America. These beliefs, which in the place of their origin had all the sanctions of religion and social custom, become, in the shadow of the white man's civilization, a pale reflection of their former selves. In time, too, they were mingled and confused with the witchcraft and ghost lore of the white man, and the tricks and delusions of the Indian conjurer. In the old plantation days they flourished vigorously, though discouraged by the "great house," and their potency was well established among the blacks and the poorer whites. Education, however, has thrown the ban of disrepute upon witchcraft and conjuration. The stern frown of the preacher, who looks upon superstition as the ally of the Evil One; the scornful sneer of the teacher, who sees in it a part of the livery of bondage, have driven this quaint combination of ancestral traditions to the remote chimney corners of old black aunties, from which it is difficult for the stranger to unearth them. Mr. Harris, in his Uncle Remus stories, has, with fine literary discrimination, collected and put into pleasing and enduring form, the plantation stories which dealt with animal lore, but so little attention has been paid to those dealing with so-called conjuration, that they seem in a fair way to disappear, without leaving a trace behind. The loss may not be very

From *Modern Culture* 13 (1901): 231–35.

great, but these vanishing traditions might furnish valuable data for the sociologist, in the future study of racial development. In writing, a few years ago, the volume entitled *The Conjure Woman*, I suspect that I was more influenced by the literary value of the material than by its sociological bearing, and therefore took, or thought I did, considerable liberty with my subject. Imagination, however, can only act upon data—one must have somewhere in his consciousness the ideas which he puts together to form a connected whole. Creative talent, of whatever grade, is, in the last analysis, only the power of rearrangement—there is nothing new under the sun. I was the more firmly impressed with this thought after I had interviewed half a dozen old women, and a genuine "conjure doctor"; for I discovered that the brilliant touches, due, I had thought, to my own imagination, were after all but dormant ideas, lodged in my childish mind by old Aunt This and old Uncle That, and awaiting only the spur of imagination to bring them again to the surface. For instance, in the story, "Hot-foot Hannibal," there figures a conjure doll with pepper feet. Those pepper feet I regarded as peculiarly my own, a purely original creation. I heard, only the other day, in North Carolina, of the consternation struck to the heart of a certain dark individual, upon finding upon his doorstep a rabbit's foot—a good omen in itself perhaps—to which a malign influence had been imparted by tying to one end of it, in the form of a cross, two small pods of red pepper!

Most of the delusions connected with this belief in conjuration grow out of mere lack of enlightenment. As primeval men saw a personality behind every natural phenomenon, and found a god or a devil in wind, rain, and hail, in lightning, and in storm, so the untaught man or woman who is assailed by an unusual ache or pain, some strenuous symptom of serious physical disorder, is prompt to accept the suggestion, which tradition approves, that some evil influence is behind his discomfort; and what more natural than to conclude that some rival in business or in love has set this force in motion?

Relics of ancestral barbarism are found among all peoples, but advanced civilization has at least shaken off the more obvious absurdities of superstition. We no longer attribute insanity to demoniac possession, nor suppose that a king's touch can cure scrofula. To many old people in the South, however, any unusual ache or pain is quite as likely to have been caused by some external evil influence as by natural causes. Tumors, sudden swellings due to inflammatory rheumatism or the bites of insects, are especially open to suspicion. Paralysis is proof positive of conjuration. If there is any doubt, the "conjure doctor" invariably removes it. The credulity of ignorance is his chief stock in trade—there is no question, when he is summoned, but that the patient has been tricked.

The means of conjuration are as simple as the indications. It is a condition of all witch stories that there must in some way be contact, either with the person, or with some object or image intended to represent the person to be affected; or, if not actual contact, at least close proximity. The charm is placed under the door-sill, or buried under the hearth, or hidden in the mattress of the person to be conjured. It may be a crude attempt to imitate the body of the victim, or it may consist merely of a bottle, or a gourd, or a little bag, containing a few rusty nails, crooked pins, or horsehairs. It may be a mysterious mixture thrown surreptitiously upon the person to be injured, or merely a line drawn across a road or path, which line it is fatal for a certain man or woman to cross. I heard of a case of a laboring man who went two miles out of his way, every morning and evening, while going to and from his work, to avoid such a line drawn for him by a certain powerful enemy.

Some of the more gruesome phases of the belief in conjuration suggest possible poisoning, a knowledge of which baleful art was once supposed to be widespread among the imported Negroes of the olden time. The blood or venom of snakes, spiders, and lizards is supposed to be employed for this purpose. The results of its administration are so peculiar, however, and so entirely improbable, that one is supposed to doubt even the initial use of poison, and figure it in as part of the same general delusion. For instance, a certain man "swelled up all over" and became "pieded," that is, pied or spotted. A white physician who was summoned thought that the man thus singularly afflicted was poisoned, but did not recognize the poison nor know the antidote. A conjure doctor, subsequently called in, was more prompt in his diagnosis. The man, he said, was poisoned with a lizard, which at that very moment was lodged somewhere in the patient's anatomy. The lizards and snakes in these stories, by the way, are not confined to the usual ducts and cavities of the human body, but seem to have freedom of movement throughout the whole structure. This lizard, according to the "doctor," would start from the man's shoulder, descend to his hand, return to the shoulder, and pass down the side of the body to the leg. When it reached the calf of the leg the lizard's head would appear right under the skin. After it had been perceptible for three days the lizard was to be cut out with a razor, or the man would die. Sure enough, the lizard manifested its presence in the appointed place at the appointed time; but the patient would not permit the surgery, and at the end of three days paid with death the penalty of his obstinacy. Old Aunt Harriet told me, with solemn earnestness, that she herself had taken a snake from her own arm, in sections, after a similar experience. Old Harriet may have been lying, but was, I imagine, merely self-deluded. Witches, prior to being burned, have often confessed their commerce with the Evil One. Why should Harriet hesitate to relate a simple personal experience which involved her in no blame whatever?

Old Uncle Jim, a shrewd, hard old sinner, and a palpable fraud, who did not, I imagine, believe in himself to any great extent, gave me some private points as to the manner in which these reptiles were thus transferred to the human system. If a snake or a lizard be killed, and a few drops of its blood be dried up on a plate or in a gourd, the person next eating or drinking from the contaminated vessel will soon become the unwilling landlord of a reptilian tenant. There are other avenues, too, by which the reptile may gain admittance; but when expelled by the conjure doctor's arts or medicines, it always leaves at the point where it entered. This belief may have originally derived its existence from the fact that certain tropical insects sometimes lay their eggs beneath the skins of animals, or even of men, from which it is difficult to expel them until the larvae are hatched. The *chico* or "jigger" of the West Indies and the Spanish Main is the most obvious example.

Old Aunt Harriet—last name uncertain, since she had borne those of her master, her mother, her putative father, and half a dozen husbands in succession, no one of which seemed to take undisputed precedence—related some very remarkable experiences. She at first manifested some reluctance to speak of conjuration, in the lore of which she was said to be well-versed; but by listening patiently to her religious experiences—she was a dreamer of dreams and a seer of visions—I was able now and then to draw a little upon her reserves of superstition, if indeed her religion itself was much more than superstition.

"W'en I wuz a gal 'bout eighteen er nineteen," she confided,

de w'ite folks use' ter sen' me ter town ter fetch vegetables. One day I met a' ole conjuh man name' Jerry Macdonal', an' he said some rough, ugly things ter me. I says, says I, "You mus' be a fool." He did n' say nothin', but jes' looked at me wid 'is evil eye. W'en I come 'long back, date ole man wuz stan'in' in de road in front er his house, an' w'en he seed me he stoop' down an' tech' de groun', jes' lack he wuz pickin' up somethin', an' den went 'long back in 'is ya'd. De ve'y minute I step' on de spot he tech', I felt a sha'p pain shoot thoo my right foot, it tu'n't under me, an' I fell down in de road. I pick' myself up' an' by de time I got home, my foot wuz swoll' up twice its nachul size. I cried an' cried an' went on, fer I knowed I'd be'n trick' by dat ole man. Dat night in my sleep a voice spoke ter me an' says: "Go an' git a plug er terbacker. Steep it in a skillet er wa'm water. Strip it lengthways, an' bin' it ter de bottom er yo' foot." I never didn' use terbacker, an' I laid dere, an' says I ter myse'f, "My Lawd, w'at is dat, w'at is dat!" Soon ez my foot got kind er easy, dat voice up an' speaks ag'in: "Go an' git a plug er ter-backer. Steep it in a skillet er wa'm water, an' bin' it ter de bottom er yo' foot." I scramble' ter my feet, got de money out er my pocket, woke up de two little boys sleepin' on de flo', an' tol' 'em ter go ter de sto' an' git me a plug er terbacker. Dey didn' want ter go, said de sto' wuz shet, an' de sto' keeper gone ter bed. But I chased 'em fu'th, an' day found' de sto' keeper an' fetch' de terbacker—dey sho' did. I soaked it in de skillet, an' stripped it 'long by degrees, till I got ter de een', w'en I boun' it under my foot an' roun' my ankle. Den I kneel' down an' prayed, an' next mawnin' de swelin' wuz all gone! Dat voice wus de Spirit er de Lawd talkin' ter me, it sho' wuz! De Lawd have mussy upon us, praise his Holy Name!

Very obviously Harriet had sprained her ankle while looking at the old man instead of watching the path, and the hot fomentation had reduced the swelling. She is not the first person to hear spirit voices in his or her own vagrant imaginings.

On another occasion, Aunt Harriet's finger swelled up "as big as a corn-cob." She at first supposed the swelling to be due to a felon. She went to old Uncle Julius Lutterloh, who told her that some one had tricked her. "My Lawd!" she exclaimed, "how did they fix my finger?" He explained that it was done while in the act of shaking hands. "Doc-tor" Julius opened the finger with a sharp knife and showed Harriet two seeds at the bottom of the incision. He instructed her to put a poultice of red onions on the wound over night, and in the morning the seeds would come out. She was then to put the two seeds in a skillet, on the right hand side of the fire-place, in a pint of water, and let them simmer nine mornings, and on the ninth morning she was to let all the water simmer out, and when the last drop should have gone, the one that put the seeds in her hand was to go out of this world! Harriet, however, did not pursue the treatment to the bitter end. The seeds, once extracted, she put into a small phial, which she corked up tightly and put carefully away in her bureau drawer. One morning she went to look at them, and one of them was gone. Shortly afterwards the other disappeared. Aunt Harriet has a theory that she had been tricked by a woman of whom her husband of that time was unduly fond, and that the faithless husband had returned the seeds to their original owner. A part of the scheme of conjuration is that the conjure doctor can remove the spell and put it back upon the one who laid it. I was unable to learn, however, of any instance where this extreme penalty had been insisted upon.

It is seldom that any of these old Negroes will admit that he or she possesses the power to conjure, though those who can remove spells are very willing to make their accomplishment known, and to exercise it for a consideration. The only professional conjure doctor whom I met was old Uncle Jim Davis, with whom I arranged a personal interview. He came to see me one evening, but almost immediately upon his arrival a minister called. The powers of light prevailed over those of darkness, and Jim was dismissed until a later time, with a commission to prepare for me a conjure "hand" or good luck charm, of which, he informed some of the children about the house, who were much interested in the pro-ceedings, I was very much in need. I subsequently secured the charm, for which, considering its potency, the small sum of silver it cost me was no extravagant outlay. It is a very small bag of roots and herbs, and, if used according to directions, is guaranteed to insure me good luck and "keep me from losing my job." The directions require it to be wet with spirits nine mornings in succession, to be carried on the person, in a pocket on the right hand side, care being taken that it does not come in contact with any tobacco. When I add that I procured, from an equally trustworthy source, a genuine graveyard rabbit's foot, I would seem to be reasonably well protected against casual misfortune. I shall not, how-ever, presume upon this immunity, and shall omit no reasonable precau-tion which the condition of my health or my affairs may render prudent.

An interesting conjure story which I heard, involves the fate of a lost voice. A certain woman's lover was enticed away by another woman, who sang very sweetly, and who, the jilted one suspected, had told lies about her. Having decided upon the method of punishment for this wicked-ness, the injured woman watched the other closely, in order to find a suitable opportunity for carrying out her purpose; but in vain, for the fortunate one, knowing of her enmity, would never speak to her or remain near her. One day the jilted woman plucked a red rose from her garden, and hid herself in the bushes near her rival's cabin. Very soon an old woman came by, who was accosted by the woman in hiding, and requested to hand the red rose to the woman of the house. The old woman, suspecting no evil, took the rose and approached the house, the other woman following her closely, but keeping herself always out of sight. When the old woman, having reached the door and called out the mistress of the house, delivered the rose as requested, the recipient thanked the giver in a loud voice, knowing the old woman to be somewhat deaf. At the moment she spoke, the woman in hiding reached up and caught her rival's voice, and clasping it tightly in her right hand, escaped, unseen, to her own cabin. At the same instant the afflicted woman missed her voice, and felt a sharp pain shoot through her left arm, just below the elbow. She at first suspected the old woman of having tricked her through the medium of the red rose, but was subsequently informed by a conjure doctor that her voice had been stolen, and that the old woman was innocent. For the pain he gave her a bottle of medicine, of which nine drops were to be applied three times a day, and rubbed in with the first two fingers of the right hand, care being taken not to let any other part of the hand touch the arm, as this would render the medicine useless. By the aid of a mirror, in which he called up her image, the conjure doctor ascertained who was the guilty person. He sought her out and charged her with the crime which she promptly denied. Being pressed, however, she admitted her guilt. The doctor insisted upon immediate restitution. She expressed her willingness, and at the same time her inability to comply—she had taken the voice, but did not possess the power to restore it. The conjure doctor was obdurate and at once placed a spell upon her which is to remain until the lost voice is restored. The case is still pending, I understand; I shall sometime take steps to find out how it terminates.

How far a story like this is original, and how far a mere reflection of familiar wonder stories, is purely a matter of speculation. When the old mammies would tell the tales of Brer Rabbit and Brer Fox to the master's children, these in turn would no doubt repeat the fairy tales which they had read in books or heard from their parents' lips. The magic mirror is as old as literature. The inability to restore the stolen voice is foreshadowed in the Arabian Nights, when the "Open Sesame" is forgotten. The act of catching the voice has a simplicity which stamps it as original, the only analogy of which I can at present think being the story of later date, of the words which were frozen silent during the extreme cold of an Arctic winter, and became audible again the following summer when they had thawed out.

Post-Bellum—Pre-Harlem

My first book, *The Conjure Woman*, was published by the Houghton Mifflin Company in 1899. It was not, strictly speaking, a novel, though it has been so called, but a collection of short stories in Negro dialect, put in the mouth of an old Negro gardener, and related by him in each instance to the same audience, which consisted of the Northern lady and gentleman who employed him. They are naïve and simple stories, dealing with alleged incidents of chattel slavery, as the old man had known it and as I had heard of it, and centering around the professional activities of old Aunt Peggy, the plantation conjure woman, and others of that ilk.

In every instance Julius had an axe to grind, for himself or his church, or some member of his family, or a white friend. The introductions to the stories, which were written in the best English I could command, developed the characters of Julius's employers and his own, and the wind-up of each story reveals the old man's ulterior purpose, which, as a general thing, is accomplished.

Most of the stories in *The Conjure Woman* had appeared in the *Atlantic Monthly* from time to time, the first story, *The Goophered Grapevine*, in the issue of August, 1887, and one of them, *The Conjurer's Revenge*, in the *Overland Monthly*. Two of them were first printed in the bound volume.

After the book had been accepted for publication, a friend of mine, the late Judge Madison W. Beacon, of Cleveland, a charter member of the Rowfant Club, suggested to the publishers a limited edition, which appeared in advance of the trade edition in an issue of one hundred and fifty numbered copies and was subscribed for almost entirely by members of the Rowfant Club and of the Cleveland bar. It was printed by the Riverside Press on large hand-made linen paper, bound in yellow buckram, with the name on the back in black letters on a white label, a very handsome and dignified volume. The trade edition was bound in brown cloth and on the front was a picture of a white-haired old Negro, flanked

From *Colophon* 2, no. 5 (1931); rpt. *Crisis* 49 (June 1931): 193–94.

on either side by a long-eared rabbit. The dust-jacket bore the same illustration.

The name of the story teller, "Uncle" Julius, and the locale of the stories, as well as the cover design, were suggestive of Mr. Harris's *Uncle Remus*, but the tales are entirely different. They are sometimes referred to as folk tales, but while they employ much of the universal machinery of wonder stories, especially the metamorphosis, with one exception, that of the first story, "The Goophered Grapevine," of which the norm was a folk tale, the stories are the fruit of my own imagination, in which respect they differ from the *Uncle Remus* stories which are avowedly folk tales.

Several subsequent editions of *The Conjure Woman* were brought out; just how many copies were sold altogether I have never informed myself, but not enough for the royalties to make me unduly rich, and in 1929, just thirty years after the first appearance of the book, a new edition was issued by Houghton Mifflin Company. It was printed from the original plates, with the very handsome title page of the limited edition, an attractive new cover in black and red, and a very flattering foreword by Colonel Joel Spingarn.

Most of my books are out of print, but I have been told that it is quite unusual for a volume of short stories which is not one of the accepted modern classics to remain on sale for so long a time.

At the time when I first broke into print seriously, no American colored writer had ever secured critical recognition except Paul Laurence Dunbar, who had won his laurels as a poet. Phillis Wheatley, a Colonial poet, had gained recognition largely because she was a slave and born in Africa, but the short story, or the novel of life and manners, had not been attempted by any one of that group.

There had been many novels dealing with slavery and the Negro. Harriet Beecher Stowe, especially in *Uncle Tom's Cabin*, had covered practically the whole subject of slavery and race admixture. George W. Cable had dwelt upon the romantic and some of the tragic features of racial contacts in Louisiana, and Judge Albion W. Tourgee, in what was one of the best sellers of his day, *A Fool's Errand*, and in his *Bricks Without Straw*, had dealt with the problems of reconstruction.

Thomas Dixon was writing the Negro down industriously and with marked popular success. Thomas Nelson Page was disguising the harshness of slavery under the mask of sentiment. The trend of public sentiment at the moment was distinctly away from the Negro. He had not developed any real political or business standing; socially he was outcast. His musical and stage successes were still for the most part unmade, and on the whole he was a small frog in a large pond, and there was a feeling of pessimism in regard to his future.

Publishers are human, and of course influenced by the opinions of their public. The firm of Houghton Mifflin, however, was unique in some respects. One of the active members of the firm was Francis J. Garrison, son of William Lloyd Garrison, from whom he had inherited his father's hatred of slavery and friendliness to the Negro. His partner, George H. Mifflin, was a liberal and generous gentleman trained in the best New England tradition. They were both friendly to my literary aspirations and became my personal friends.

But the member of their staff who was of most assistance to me in publishing my first book was Walter Hines Page, later ambassador to England under President Wilson, and at that time editor of the *Atlantic Monthly*, as well as literary adviser for the publishing house, himself a liberalized Southerner, who derived from the same part of the South where the stories in *The Conjure Woman* are located, and where I passed my adolescent years. He was a graduate of Macon College, a fellow of Johns Hopkins University, had been attached to the staff of the *Forum* and the *New York Evening Post*, and was as broad-minded a Southerner as it was ever my good fortune to meet.

Three of the *Atlantic* editors wrote novels dealing with race problems—William Dean Howells in *An Imperative Duty*, Bliss Perry in *The Plated City*, and Mr. Page in *The Autobiography of Nicholas Worth*.

The first of my conjure stories had been accepted for the *Atlantic* by Thomas Bailey Aldrich, the genial auburn-haired poet who at that time presided over the editorial desk. My relations with him, for the short time they lasted, were most cordial and friendly.

Later on I submitted to Mr. Page several stories of post-war life among the colored people which the *Atlantic* published, and still later the manuscript of a novel. The novel was rejected, and was subsequently rewritten and published by Houghton Mifflin under the title of *The House Behind the Cedars*. Mr. Page, who had read the manuscript, softened its rejection by the suggestion that perhaps a collection of the conjure stories might be undertaken by the firm with a better prospect of success. I was in the hands of my friends, and submitted the collection. After some omissions and additions, all at the advice of Mr. Page, the book was accepted and announced as *The Conjure Woman*, in 1899, and I enjoyed all the delights of proof-reading and the other pleasant emotions attending the publication of a first book. Mr. Page, Mr. Garrison and Mr. Mifflin vied with each other in helping to make our joint venture a literary and financial success.

The book was favorably reviewed by literary critics. If I may be pardoned one quotation, William Dean Howells, always the friend of the aspiring author, in an article published in the *Atlantic Monthly* for May, 1900, wrote:

"The stories of *The Conjure Woman* have a wild, indigenous poetry, the creation of sincere and original imagination, which is imparted with a tender humorousness and a very artistic reticence. As far as his race is concerned, or his sixteenth part of a race, it does not greatly matter whether Mr. Chesnutt invented their motives, or found them, as he feigns, among his distant cousins of the Southern cabins. In either case the wonder of their beauty is the same, and whatever is primitive and sylvan or campestral in the reader's heart is touched by the spells thrown on the simple black lives in these enchanting tales. Character, the most precious thing in fiction, is faithfully portrayed."

Imagine the thrill with which a new author would read such an encomium from such a source!

From the publisher's standpoint, the book proved a modest success. This was by no means a foregone conclusion, even assuming its literary merit and the publisher's imprint, for reasons which I shall try to make clear.

I have been referred to as the "first Negro novelist," meaning, of course, in the United States; Pushkin in Russia and the two Dumas in France had produced a large body of popular fiction. At that time a literary work by an American of acknowledged color was a doubtful experiment, both for the writer and for the publisher, entirely apart from its intrinsic merit. Indeed, my race was never mentioned by the publishers in announcing or advertising the book. From my own viewpoint it was a personal matter. It never occurred to me to claim any merit because of it, and I have always resented the denial of anything on account of it. My colored friends, however, with a very natural and laudable zeal for the race, with which I found no fault, saw to it that the fact was not overlooked, and I have before me a copy of a letter written by one of them to the editor of the *Atlanta Constitution,* which had published a favorable review of the book, accompanied by my portrait, chiding him because the reviewer had not referred to my color.

A woman critic of Jackson, Mississippi, questioning what she called the rumor as to my race, added, "Some people claim that Alexander Dumas, author of *The Count of Monte Cristo* and *The Three Musketeers,* was a colored man. This is obviously untrue, because no Negro could possibly have written these books"—a pontifical announcement which would seem to settle the question definitely, despite the historical evidence to the contrary.

While *The Conjure Woman* was in the press, the *Atlantic* published a short story of mine called "The Wife of His Youth" which attracted wide attention. James McArthur, at that time connected with the *Critic,* later with *Harper's,* in talking one day with Mr. Page, learned of my race and requested leave to mention it as a matter of interest to the literary public. Mr. Page demurred at first on the ground that such an announcement might be harmful to the success of my forthcoming book, but finally consented, and Mr. McArthur mentioned the fact in the *Critic,* referring to me as a "mulatto."

As a matter of fact, substantially all of my writings, with the exception of *The Conjure Woman,* have dealt with the problems of people of mixed blood, which, while in the main the same as those of the true Negro, are in some instances and in some respects much more complex and difficult of treatment, in fiction as in life.

I have lived to see, after twenty years or more, a marked change in the attitude of publishers and the reading public in regard to the Negro in fiction. The development of Harlem, with its large colored population in all shades, from ivory to ebony, of all degrees of culture, from doctors of philosophy to the lowest grade of illiteracy; its various origins, North American, South American, West Indian and African; its morals ranging from the highest to the most debased; with the vivid life of its cabarets, dance halls and theatres; with its ambitious business and professional men, its actors, singers, novelists and poets, its aspirations and demands for equality—without which any people would merit only contempt— presented a new field for literary exploration which of recent years has been cultivated assiduously.

One of the first of the New York writers to appreciate the possibilities of Harlem for literary purposes was Carl Van Vechten, whose novel *Nigger Heaven* was rather severely criticized by some of the colored intellectuals as a libel on the race, while others of them praised it highly. I was prejudiced in its favor for reasons which those who have read the book will understand. I found it a vivid and interesting story which presented some new and better type of Negroes and treated them sympathetically.

The Negro novel, whether written by white or colored authors, has gone so much farther now in the respects in which it was criticized that *Nigger Heaven,* in comparison with some of these later productions, would be almost as mild as a Sunday School tract compared to *The Adventures of Fanny Hill*. Several of these novels, by white and colored authors alike, reveal such an intimate and meticulous familiarity with the baser aspects of Negro life, North and South, that one is inclined to wonder how and from what social sub-sewers they gathered their information. With the exception of one or two of the earlier ones, the heroine of the novel is never chaste, though for the matter of that few post-Victorian heroines are, and most of the male characters are likewise weaklings or worse.

I have in mind a recent novel, brilliantly written by a gifted black author, in which, to my memory, there is not a single decent character, male or female. These books are written primarily for white readers, as it is extremely doubtful whether a novel, however good, could succeed financially on its sales to colored readers alone. But it seems to me that a body of twelve million people, struggling upward slowly but surely from a lowly estate, must present all along the line of its advancement many situations full of dramatic interest, ranging from farce to tragedy, with many admirable types worthy of delineation.

Caste, a principal motive of fiction from Richardson down through the Victorian epoch, has pretty well vanished among white Americans. Between the whites and the Negroes it is acute, and is bound to develop an increasingly difficult complexity, while among the colored people themselves it is just beginning to appear.

Negro writers no longer have any difficulty in finding publishers. Their race is no longer a detriment but a good selling point, and publishers are seeking their books, sometimes, I am inclined to think, with less regard for quality than in the case of white writers. To date, colored writers have felt restricted for subjects to their own particular group, but there is every reason to hope that in the future, with proper encouragement, they will make an increasingly valuable contribution to literature, and perhaps produce chronicles of life comparable to those of Dostoevski, Dumas, Dickens or Balzac.

Part 3

THE CRITICS

Introduction

One of the decisive events in Chesnutt's literary career was the appearance in 1900 of William Dean Howells's celebratory essay "Mr. Charles W. Chesnutt's Stories" in the *Atlantic Monthly*. Subsequent criticism written during Chesnutt's lifetime was noticeably more guarded than Howells's ringing tribute, however, and by the 1930s Chesnutt had virtually disappeared under the shadow of the Harlem Renaissance. Critics of the '30s and '40s who did not dismiss him entirely tended to regard Chesnutt as, in J. Saunders Redding's words, "a transitional figure" linking the post–Civil War era to the artistic ferment of Harlem in the 1920s. Chesnutt's daughter, Helen, revived considerable interest in her father's literary achievement with the publication of *Charles Waddell Chesnutt: Pioneer of the Color Line* in 1952, and a steady flow of important commentary on his life and work has followed ever since. Groundbreaking archival and interpretive work by scholars such as Sylvia Lyons Render, Noel J. Heermance, Robert Hemenway, and Frances Richardson Keller sustained Chesnutt studies through the 1960s and '70s, two decades of fruitful research that culminated with the publication of William L. Andrews's authoritative 1980 study, *The Literary Career of Charles W. Chesnutt*, part of which is reprinted here.

Since the appearance of Andrews's book, interest in Chesnutt's short fiction has steadily gained momentum. Critics such as Robert Stepto, John Edgar Wideman, Werner Sollors, Lorne Fienberg, Eric Selinger, Eugene Terry, Richard Brodhead, Robert Nowatzki, and Craig Werner have introduced compelling new readings of the stories, all of which deserve to be represented in an overview of Chesnutt criticism. Rather than delve superficially into such a variety of advanced approaches, however, I have decided to reproduce extended excerpts from only a few particularly significant critical works. One of these is Houston A. Baker Jr.'s *Modernism and the Harlem Renaissance*, a book that has helped to clarify Chesnutt's centrality to the African-American tradition in fiction by connecting the subversive capacity of his art to the concept of literary modernism. Building on Baker's understanding of the trickster motif in African-American rhetorical performance, Eric Sundquist has introduced a new level of sophistication to Chesnutt studies in *To Wake the Nations: Race in the Making of American Literature,* an excerpt of which also appears in this section. Part 3 ends with Ben Slote's brilliant essay on the intricate iconography of "The Goophered Grapevine," a story whose apparent gratification of racist impulses presents a unique set of interpretive and pedagogic challenges. In addressing the ambivalent racial dynamics everywhere at play in Chesnutt's fiction, Slote's essay raises a set of issues that critics have only begun to consider, issues that, once engaged, promise to sustain a vital interest in his stories well into the future.

William Dean Howells

The critical reader of the story called "The Wife of His Youth," which appeared in these pages two years ago, must have noticed uncommon traits in what was altogether a remarkable piece of work. The first was the novelty of the material; for the writer dealt not only with people who were not white, but with people who were not black enough to contrast grotesquely with white people,—who in fact were of that near approach to the ordinary American in race and color which leaves, at the last degree, everyone but the connoisseur in doubt whether they are Anglo-Saxon or Anglo-African. Quite as striking as this novelty of the material was the author's thorough mastery of it, and his unerring knowledge of the life he had chosen in its peculiar racial characteristics. But above all, the story was notable for the passionless handling of a phase of our common life which is tense with potential tragedy; for the attitude, almost ironical, in which the artist observes the play of contesting emotions in the drama under his eyes; and for his apparently reluctant, apparently helpless consent to let the spectator know his real feeling in the matter. Anyone accustomed to study methods in fiction, to distinguish between good and bad art, to feel the joy which the delicate skill possible only from a love of truth can give, must have known a high pleasure in the quiet self-restraint of the performance; and such a reader would probably have decided that the social situation in the piece was studied wholly from the outside, by an observer with special opportunities for knowing it, who was, as it were, surprised into final sympathy.

Now, however, it is known that the author of this story is of negro blood,—diluted, indeed, in such measure that if he did not admit this descent few would imagine it, but still quite of that middle world which lies next, though wholly outside, our own. Since his first story appeared he has contributed several others to these pages, and he now makes a showing palpable to criticism in a volume called *The Wife of His Youth and*

From "Mr. Charles W. Chesnutt's Stories," *Atlantic Monthly* 85 (May 1900: 699–700.

Other Stories of the Color Line; a volume of Southern sketches called *The Conjure Woman;* and a short life of Frederick Douglass, in the Beacon Series of Biographies. The last is a simple, solid, straight piece of work, not remarkable above many other biographical studies by people entirely white, and yet important as the work of a man not entirely white treating of a great man of his inalienable race. But the volumes of fiction *are* remarkable above many, above most short stories by people entirely white, and would be worthy of unusual notice if they were not the work of a man not entirely white.

It is not from their racial interest that we would first wish to speak of them, though that must have a very great and very just claim upon the critic. It is much more simply and directly, as works of art, that they make their appeal, and we must allow the force of this quite independently of the other interest. Yet it cannot always be allowed. There are times in each of the stories of the first volume when the simplicity lapses, and the effect is of a weak and uninstructed touch. There are other times when the attitude, severely impartial and studiously aloof, accuses itself of a little pompousness. There are still other times when the literature is a little too ornate for beauty, and the diction is journalistic, reporteristic. But it is right to add that these are the exceptional times, and that for far the greatest part Mr. Chesnutt seems to know quite as well what he wants to do in a given case as Maupassant, or Tourguénief, or Mr. James, or Miss Jewett, or Miss Wilkins, in other given cases, and has done it with an art of kindred quiet and force. He belongs, in other words, to the good school, the only school, all aberrations from nature being so much truancy and anarchy. He sees his people very clearly, very justly, and he shows them as he sees them, leaving the reader to divine the depth of his feeling for them. He touches all the stops, and with equal delicacy in stories of real tragedy and comedy and pathos, so that it would be hard to say which is the finest in such admirably rendered effects as "The Web of Circumstance," "The Bouquet," and "Uncle Wellington's Wives." In some others the comedy degenerates into satire, with a look in the reader's direction which the author's friends must deplore.

As these stories are of our own time and country, and as there is not a swashbuckler of the seventeenth century, or a sentimentalist of this, or a princess of an imaginary kingdom, in any of them, they will possibly not reach half a million readers in six months, but in twelve months possibly more readers will remember them than if they had reached the half million. They are new and fresh and strong, as life always is, and fable never is; and the stories of *The Conjure Woman* have a wild, indigenous poetry, the creation of sincere and original imagination, which is imparted with a tender humorousness and a very artistic reticence. As far as his race is concerned, or his sixteenth part of a race, it does not greatly matter whether Mr. Chesnutt invented their motives, or found them, as he feigns, among his distant cousins of the Southern cabins. In either case, the wonder of their beauty is the same; and whatever is primitive and sylvan or campestral in the reader's heart is touched by the spells thrown on the simple black lives in these enchanting tales. Character, the most precious thing in fiction, is as faithfully portrayed against the poetic background as in the setting of the *Stories of the Color Line*.

Yet these stories, after all, are Mr. Chesnutt's most important work, whether we consider them merely as realistic fiction, apart from their author, or as studies of that middle world of which he is naturally and voluntarily a citizen. We had known the nethermost world of the grotesque and comical negro and the terrible and tragic negro through the white observer on the outside, and black character in its lyrical moods we had known from such an inside witness as Mr. Paul Dunbar; but it had remained for Mr. Chesnutt to acquaint us with those regions where the paler shades dwell as hopelessly, with relation to ourselves, as the blackest negro. He has not shown the dwellers there as very different from ourselves. They have within their own circles the same social ambitions and prejudices; they intrigue and truckle and crawl, and are snobs, like ourselves, both the snobs that snub and the snobs that are snubbed. We may choose to think them droll in their parody of pure white society, but perhaps it would be wiser to recognize that they are like us because they are of our blood by more than half, or three quarters, or nine tenths. It is not, in such cases, their negro blood that characterizes them; but it is their negro blood that excludes them, and that will imaginably fortify them and exalt them. Bound in that sad solidarity from which there is no hope of entrance into polite white society for them, they may create a civilization of their own, which need not lack the highest quality. They need not be ashamed of the race from which they have sprung, and whose exile they share; for in many of the arts it has already shown, during a single generation of freedom, gifts which slavery apparently only obscured. With Mr. Booker T. Washington the first American orator of our time, fresh upon the time of Frederick Douglass; with Mr. Dunbar among the truest of our poets; with Mr. Tanner, a black American, among the only three Americans from whom the

French government ever bought a picture, Mr. Chesnutt may well be willing to own his color.

But that is his personal affair. Our more universal interest in him arises from the more than promise he has given in a department of literature where Americans hold the foremost place. In this there is, happily, no color line; and if he has it in him to go forward on the way which he has traced for himself, to be true to life as he has known it, to deny himself the glories of the cheap success which awaits the charlatan in fiction, one of the places at the top is open to him. He has sounded a fresh note, boldly, not blatantly, and he has won the ear of the more intelligent public.

J. Saunders Redding

Charles W. Chesnutt is a transitional figure. He drew together the various post-Civil War tendencies in Negro creative literature and translated them into the most worthy prose fiction that the Negro had produced.

Chesnutt's career began with the publication of a series of stories, starting in the *Atlantic Monthly* in 1887. In 1899 these stories were collected and issued as *The Conjure Woman*. The book's reception as the work of a white writer indicates much as to Chesnutt's earlier artistic objectivity and, more important perhaps, signifies that he was judged by the standards of his white contemporaries. By these standards *The Conjure Woman* is successful. In one stroke Chesnutt had achieved what others had striven for interminably. Written around a central framework, the care with which the stories are done bespeaks the writer's artistic sincerity. The tales, concerned with the deeds and misdeeds of a conjure woman, are connected with each other in such a way as to give them more than the superficial unity which the framework supplies. The plan is very simple. Uncle Julius, a frosty-headed Negro who has lived through and absorbed all the romance and reality of slavery, tells the seven folk tales to a northern white couple recently moved to North Carolina.

Though it was generally known that Chesnutt was a Negro after the publication of *The Wife of His Youth* in 1899, he nevertheless continued to write occasional stories that gave no indication of his color. The satirical gem, "Baxter's Procrustes," is the best known of these. But after a series of stories and novels dealing with the Negro and the color line and its problems, most of Chesnutt's objective stories seem forced and unnatural, wan and vigorless, mere water colors. For sheer accomplishment in work of this kind he never surpassed *The Conjure Woman*, and none of his later stories ever equaled the folk tale "The Gray Wolf's Ha'nt," that dark and cruel tragedy of jealousy and love. Nearly all the stories of this

From *To Make a Poet Black* (Chapel Hill: University of North Carolina Press, 1939), 68–71.

first collection are tragic with the fatal consequences of human actions and prejudices. It is not the weak pseudo-tragedy of propaganda, it is not pathos and tears in which Chesnutt deals—it is the fundamental stuff of life translated into the folk terms of a people who knew true tragedy.

Chesnutt's first volume proved two important points. It proved that the Negro could be made the subject of serious esthetic treatment without the interference of propaganda; and it proved that the Negro creative artist could submerge himself objectively in his material. It must not be thought, however, that the tradition of buffoonery was broken by *The Conjure Woman*. The buffoon had two faces. He grinned and danced and capered as a minstrel Sambo and in the stories of certain popular authors, while Joe Chandler Harris saw the other face, the blandly kind and childish smile, the improvident generosity and loyalty. But he was still a Negro, lazy, ignorant, dependent. Both faces showed him as a woefully inferior being, and that was the very core of the tradition. Like a Jewish actor in pre-Christian Rome, he might be the instrument of tragedy, but he was never tragic. Beneath the mask there grinned the Negro.

After several years of teaching in North Carolina, Charles Chesnutt returned to his home in Cleveland in 1887. The effect upon him of his return to a way of life that had grown strange was immediate. In the South the distance between himself and the majority of Negroes with whom he came into contact was immeasurable. He was not wedded to them by the bonds of common circumstance, environment, and habit. He understood them, but he did not feel a blood-warm kinship to their earth, nor a destiny common to their destiny. The objectivity of *The Conjure Woman* argues the gulf. His sympathetic understanding of southern Negroes, which never faltered, was in part at least the product of the very distance at which he stood from them. In Cleveland he was home again among the people of the color line, his people. He knew again the habits, problems, vagaries of life, his life, along the color line. Kinship here was real and inescapable. He had to shift his point of view, to feel the artist merge into the man. The title of his second book, *The Wife of his Youth and Other Stories of the Color Line*, is symptomatic. And when he appends the following to the story "The Web of Circumstance," we hear the soul cry of the Negro.

"We are told, when the cycle of years has rolled around, there is to be another golden age, when all men will dwell together in love and harmony—God speed the day … but give us here and there, and now and then, some little foretaste of this golden age, that we may the more patiently and hopefully await its coming."

The struggle between Chesnutt the artist and Chesnutt the man (not immediately resolved) is evident in *The Wife of His Youth*. In these stories Chesnutt discards folk material to deal with the lives of a certain Negro type in Cleveland, the "Groveland" of his stories. These people represent the special and important group of Negroes with a large admixture of white blood. Because the peculiar situation of the near-whites was (and is) considered ideal for the purposes of propaganda, their lives had been used by nearly all the Negro novelists prior to Dunbar. This put upon such characters a certain stamp, and in that stamp lay danger for Chesnutt the artist.

The moods in which Chesnutt approaches his material are puzzling. In only a few of these stories is the reader sure of the author's point of view, his convictions. In "A Matter of Principle," for an instance, a story of the color line in which the daughter of a well-to-do quadroon family loses a brilliant marriage because her father mistakes a stout, black gentleman for the lover whom he has never seen—what is the author's point of view? Based on the tragic absurdity of colorphobia, the story is a comedy of manners in the Molière sense. But what is Chesnutt's conviction as an artist? Does he sympathize with the existence of a color caste within the race? Is he holding his characters up to ridicule? Of what is he trying to convince us? In this and other stories one seems always at the point of making a discovery about the author, but the discovery never matures. The truth seems to be that in 1899, more than ten years after his return to Cleveland, Chesnutt's struggle was still in progress. He still was not sure what his attitude should be.

The title story, "The Wife of his Youth," is an exception. The delicacy of its mood, the tempered sharpness of its point, and the subtle simplicity of characterization remind one of Hawthorne. Indeed, it might have been conceived and executed by the author of *Twice Told Tales*. The story is of a mulatto who, married to a dark-skinned Negro woman as a very young man in slavery, escapes to the North, acquires an education, and forgets his black wife. After the emancipation, in the midst of a celebration on the eve of the mulatto's marriage to a woman of the color line, the wife of his youth appears, and he acknowledges her before the gathering of near-white friends. It is not character that is of most interest here. The characters are flat, two-dimensional. Situation, circumstance—and beyond these, the whole complex social structure—draw our attention. Only Chesnutt's brooding sympathy for the problems present in the society of which he writes makes the story at all possible. One feels here something more of his personality than that which ordinarily belongs to creative writing. One finds here a key to him, the ever-coiling spring of his future creativeness.

William L. Andrews

In a smaller group of color line stories, Chesnutt restrained his didactic predilection in favor of a more disinterested, journalistic tone befitting a social observer and commentator. The social phenomena observed in such stories as "The Bouquet" or "The Web of Circumstance" or "The Sheriff's Children" bear witness to problems inherent in the Afro-American's situation in the postwar South which could not be alleviated simply by the more steadfast practice of the middle-class work ethic by blacks. Exacerbating the problem of Afro-American progress in the New South were white prejudices, suspicions, envy, and indifference toward blacks, all of which were rapidly becoming institutionalized in varying forms of racial discrimination. The more obvious and well-publicized aspect of the New South color line, that which stretched around the voting booth, Chesnutt did not take up in his earliest short stories of social analysis. Instead, he focused on manifestations of color bias in less politically sensitive areas of southern civil and social activity in order to point up the extent of the color line problem without embroiling it in the fires of political controversy. Notoriety as a black polemicist in literature, a "protest" writer against racial injustice, would not open the doors of the popular magazines and publishing houses further to him. Somehow Chesnutt had to adapt his most original but most potentially controversial subject matter, the caste system in the South, to the exigencies of the genteel white literary market. Somehow he had to make his revisionist point without sounding like a controversialist. For the most prestigious of the belletristic magazines he had to put aside the didactic tone, schematic plots, and simplistic resolutions of his color line *exempla*. At the same time, he could not indulge in fictionalized catalogs of social abuses nor could he give way to an unprecedented outspokenness in defense of southern blacks and in criticism of southern whites. If he was to win a hearing for his analysis of the black man's civil

Reprinted by permission of Louisiana State University Press from *The Literary Career of Charles W. Chesnutt* by William L. Andrews. Copyright © 1980 by Louisiana State University Press.

and social situation in a racist New South, he had to discover a popular mode of the short story congenial to his literary temperament and thematic purposes. This was the artistic dilemma facing Chesnutt when he first began to experiment in color line stories of social comment and incipient protest....

In "The Bouquet" Chesnutt divided his attention between the delineation of the segregated pattern of small-town southern life and the recounting of a pathetic, almost sentimental tale of a black schoolgirl's adoring love for her beautiful white teacher, a flower of southern womanhood who wilts in death in the course of the story.[1] The social analysis in the story is not detailed; examples of discrimination against blacks are mentioned without special highlighting from the author. Loss of caste for aristocrats who associate with blacks, segregation in church services, and resistance to black education in general are features of southern life and thought which provide the social background and influence the action of "The Bouquet." Occasionally Chesnutt dips into sarcasm at the expense of the schoolteacher's mother, one of the many unreconstructed aristocrats in his color line fiction, but he also speaks with tolerant comprehension of the causes of her bigoted behavior, leaving the reader to judge her as he wishes. At the end of the story, when Sophy Tucker is excluded from the funeral of her idolized teacher, Miss Myrover, Chesnutt draws the threads of his tale together in an emotionally charged denouement. The Old South racial credo expounded by Mrs. Myrover finds its social manifestation in the segregated funeral service which ostracizes Sophy, the unoffending representative of the New Negro generation in the story. Thus the partially enlightened noblesse oblige of Miss Myrover, ambivalently eulogized by Chesnutt, is undone by her benighted mother, whose survival past her daughter's death testifies to the frailty of New South progressivism and the vitality of the old caste spirit.

The Wilmington, North Carolina, *Messenger* winced at the indictment of "Wellington's" small-town cruelty in "The Bouquet" and denounced Chesnutt for distorting the social relationship between the races in the contemporary South.[2] On the other hand, William Dean Howells pronounced himself "touched" by the sentimental strategy of "The Bouquet."[3] A more distanced critical perspective, however, will find too little to recommend in it. The firmness of Chesnutt's moral convictions tends to force the literary issue. The characters in "The Bouquet" are type-ridden, particularly Sophy, the black schoolgirl, who is little more than a diminutive personification of the Afro-American as devoted, patient, long-suffering, and wholly self-forgetful. Such stereotypical characteristics do not make her an interesting figure, but in the situation in which she is placed, this extreme simplification of her nature does make her eminently pitiable. And this seems to be the author's paramount purpose in the story, to evoke pity from a situation of patent injustice. Because Sophy is an innocent child, not an "uppity" black adult, no justification can be mustered for Mrs. Myrover's prejudice or Wellington's segregation customs. What more trenchant comment on the effect of the color line could be posed for an American reading audience already primed by domestic childhood literature to sentimentalize and idealize children? Segregation is not pictured as a socioeconomic system in "The Bouquet." It is a moral blight which ultimately thwarts the love of little children. No wonder the *Atlantic* chose this story to run as an advertisement for *The Wife of His Youth*. It had a social timeliness and muted sensational appeal which at the same time was sugared to the tastes of genteel readers by use of a simple plot turning on matters of the heart toward an almost lachrymose conclusion. Thus "The Bouquet" shows one way Chesnutt tried early in his career to reconcile serious social comment and purpose with popular reader expectations. If the story seems more successful in arousing strong feelings than in dispassionately analyzing color line conditions, it foreshadows the uneasy yoking of melodramatic scene and social protest rhetoric which pervades Chesnutt's later and longer color line fiction.

While "The Bouquet" evidences Chesnutt's affinity for sentimentality in his protest-oriented stories, "The Web of Circumstance," the concluding story in *The Wife of His Youth*, reveals the influence of the "new realists" on Chesnutt's approach to the fiction of social analysis. Although most of Chesnutt's most memorable color line stories follow Howells' emphasis on the accurate portrayal of ordinary experience with special concern for the social and moral consequences of human choice, the theme of determinism and atavism which emerge from "The Web of Circumstance" imply Chesnutt's reading of naturalistic authors. The main character of his story, Ben Davis, initially resembles Nimbus Ware of Albion Tourgée's *Bricks Without Straw* (1880). Both men are industrious, self-reliant, prosperous black men in the postwar South, the leaders of a potential black middle class. But both men's impolitic views about black self-determination and white reparations stir up white resentment. Nimbus Ware is removed from the scene by the Ku Klux Klan, in keeping with the realities of southern life during the Reconstruction period which Tourgée chronicled. Ben Davis, on the other hand, is separated from his property, his family, and finally his hope by the influence of less visible forces. Both Tourgée and Chesnutt denigrate "Southern justice" in these stories, but for Chesnutt a truthful dramatization of the black man's chances in the white man's courts could not proceed upon the assumption that old villains like the Klan remained the chief obstacles between the New Negro and his rights. In "The Web of Circumstance" Ben Davis is not up against a malign, identifiable foe. He is done in by a concatenation of random circumstances: the jealousy of his employee, the unfaithfulness of his wife, the ambition of a prosecutor, the race prejudice of a judge, the blind despair of his own subsequent criminal status, the degrading companionship of imprisoned, brutalized men, and finally, the misinterpretation of an unthinking act, which causes a white man to shoot him down.

The thread of circumstance which entangles Davis and his family in a web of powerlessness, poverty, and eventual destruction is supported in several crucial instances by color prejudice. The theft of the whip which leads to Davis' trial, wrongful conviction, and imprisonment appears to be motivated by intra-racial envy, but the "evidence" which convicts him and which governs the judge's unduly harsh sentence arises out of white fear of black upward mobility. For sounding hardly more radical than Booker T. Washington in his counsel to blacks that they support their own enterprises, accumulate capital, and acquire property, Davis is slandered as an anarchist, a nihilist, a communist, and a revolutionary by the prosecutor in his trial. After white killers and forgers receive mercy at the bench, Davis, whose "crime" is the avowed pursuit of black economic power in a white supremacist system, gets five years for stealing a whip.

Once his protagonist is incarcerated, the oppressive influence of environment becomes Chesnutt's major theme. "After five years of unrequited toil, and unspeakable hardship in convict camps,—five years of slaving by the side of human brutes, and of nightly herding with them in vermin-haunted huts,—Ben Davis had become like them." When Davis returns home it is not to resume his leadership role among his people, as Nimbus Ware does after working on a prison crew in *Bricks Without Straw*. Less hopeful than Tourgée about his hero's recuperative powers, Chesnutt presses the naturalistic implications of Davis' tragedy by surveying the fate of his family, all of them victims of the chain of events which they could control even less than Davis. Davis' ignominious death, the result of a combination of coincidence, misleading appearances, and automatic racial suppositions, brings Chesnutt to the end of this most pessimistic of his color line stories. Told with detached objectivity and an absence of the authorial interruptions which mar the pace of his other socioeconomic tales, "The Web of Circumstance" does not pile up the "scientific" detail of a Norris or a Dreiser. But as a record of the way in which economic, social, and psychological conditions can unite to throttle human aspirations and quash human dignity, the story stands firmly in the naturalistic tradition. The logic of events in the story may not seem always compellingly naturalistic, but then the story seems more concerned with using some of the premises of naturalism to make a social point than merely to demonstrate naturalistic conclusions for their own sake.

Like Hamlin Garland, Mary E. Wilkins Freeman, and the early Jack London, all of whom infused regionalism with a new critical realism, Chesnutt took a familiar regional character—the southern Negro— located in a familiar local color setting—the southern small town—and created a socioeconomic case study. He made "The Web of Circum- stance" illustrate the impossibility of black assimilation into the fore- front of southern economic life so long as racism continued to poison the social atmosphere. While reporting how color prejudice permeates the total environment of the black man, ready at the rise of fortuitous circumstance to crush his economic aspirations, Chesnutt implicitly admitted his own reservations to his much-declaimed faith in the mid- dle-class work ethic. Yet he would not give voice to this nay-saying sen- timent. On the contrary, as if realizing the despairing drift of his story, Chesnutt dropped the pose of the impartial reporter and practitioner of the new analytic realism at the end of "The Web of Circumstance." Instead, the story concludes with the following prayer, delivered by the author as he looks past Davis' tragedy toward a "golden age" of social "peace and righteousness": "Let not the shining thread of hope become so enmeshed in the web of circumstance that we lose sight of it; but give us here and there, and now and then, some little foretaste of this golden age, that we may patiently and hopefully await its coming!"

Through this exhortatory coda, urging patience, not despair in the face of Davis' tragic example, Chesnutt drew back from the dispiriting conclusions which a strictly naturalistic representation of the Afro- American's situation demanded. His idea of the writer's moral responsi- bility balked at the absolute detachment of the "scientific" realist. His color line fiction would never allow his reader to lose sight of "the shin- ing thread of hope." In "The Web of Circumstance," unfortunately, that thread of hope hangs by a rhetorical tack at the conclusion, detracting from the aesthetic integrity of the story as a work of new realism. This structural weakness seems to have impressed Chesnutt, for he never wrote another naturalistic short story. The aesthetic problem raised in "The Web of Circumstance"—reconciling the new realist's method to Chesnutt's moral aims—would return in Chesnutt's last novel. But in the interval, picturing the Afro-American situation as hopelessly determined precluded the possibility of choice and change, at least on the individual level, and such possibilities were what Chesnutt had designed his writing to encourage, not deny.

Because "The Sheriff's Children" allows for these possibilities within a southern context as oppressive and racist as that of "The Web of Circumstance," its significance among Chesnutt's pioneering protest-oriented color line stories is central. Among his short fiction, "The Sheriff's Children"[4] constitutes Chesnutt's boldest arraignment of the South, both Old and New, for its sins of omission and commission against black people. The bitterness of the mulatto protagonist in this story and his hopeless estimate of his situation in postwar America represents the extremest statement of the southern Afro-American's case that Chesnutt ever mustered in his color line fiction. Nevertheless, the focal question in this, Chesnutt's quintessential "problem" story, is not the abuses suffered by the black man in the New South, which is the theme of protest stories like "The Bouquet" or "The Web of Circumstance." What makes "The Sheriff's Children" both unique among Chesnutt's race problem stories and prophetic of his later problem novels is its redirection of the southern color question, so that the problem of the black man's presence in the South is laid before the southern white man, who, as "The Sheriff's Children" argues, must recognize his past complicity and present responsibility if "the problem" is ever to be solved.

"The Sheriff's Children" is set in Chesnutt's typical small town, the provincial hamlet of Troy, North Carolina, not much different from the Patesvilles and Wellingtons which are the loci of Chesnutt's most famous protest short stories and novels. Exemplifying the small-town South in the postbellum era, Troy is bereft of the romantic accoutrements of the Old South and untouched by the instruments of New South enterprise and progressivism. Time seems to stand still in the decaying pastoral world of Troy, as is usual in the typical southern town of Chesnutt's color line fiction. Within such a protective stasis, most of the townspeople exist in a world of their own myths and memories, to be roused only by the intrusion of dynamic forces from the outside.

Reminiscent of the unromantic depiction of small-town folk in *Huckleberry Finn*, Chesnutt's gallery of background characters in his story is realistically sketched. The denizens of Troy are summoned before the reader as "bearded men in straw hats and blue homespun shirts, and butternut trousers of great amplitude of material and vagueness of outline; women in homespun frocks and slat-bonnets, with faces as expressionless as the dreary sandhills which gave them a meagre sustenance." These occupants of the southern deserted village set the mood of "The Sheriff's Children." The general ambience of lethargy and cultural stagnation which so oppressed Chesnutt while he labored in the Troys and Patesvilles of postwar North Carolina signifies in "The Sheriff's Children" the atrophy of the moral fiber of the New South.

In the midst of this "social corpse" of a town, Chesnutt elevates one man of awareness and distinction, Sheriff Campbell, scion of an aristocratic family, a former Confederate officer, a man of some intellectual sophistication and progressive bent. His job it is to protect "a strange mulatto," suspected of murdering a white man, from a local lynch mob. The sheriff proves equal to the task. "I'm sheriff of this county; I know my duty, and I mean to do it," Campbell proclaims confidently, and through his victory of will over the mob of ex-rebels, the story reaches a preliminary climax. For once, the forces of law and decency prevail over those of racial enmity and violence in the South of Chesnutt's fiction. Under the moderating guardian care of one of the "best people" of the New South, a reconstructed aristocrat, civil rehabilitation under law appears to be progressing. True justice seems available to the Afro-American because the southern aristocracy has extended its sense of noblesse oblige to the freedman's legal rights.

This is all very well as far as it goes, but the point of "The Sheriff's Children" is to show that Campbell's duty-consciousness to the Afro-American in his custody has never gone far enough. Chesnutt as narrator hints as much when he states that Campbell "knew what his duty was, as sheriff, perhaps more clearly than he had apprehended it in other passages of his life." Tom, the mulatto, forces the "duty" issue to the forefront of the story when, after revealing to his captor that he is the sheriff's illegitimate slave-born son, he demands, " 'What father's duty have you ever performed for me?' " The answer the sheriff must give is morally damning. Many years before he had sired a son by one of his slaves and then sold them both to avoid the onus of moral and paternal responsibility. But, as it so often turns out in Chesnutt's fiction, the past will not stay past. "The Sheriff's Children" is but the first of many

Chesnutt "parables" in which the individual and collective moral sins of the southern fathers haunt the New South like a dark incubus, like Tom the outraged and vengeful mulatto. The purpose of "The Sheriff's Children"—and of most of Chesnutt's later studies of the New South race problem—is to force the morally culpable white southerner, symbolized at his best in Campbell, to realize that he cannot easily "shake off the consequences of his sin" against the black man. Nor will official recognition of the Afro-American's legal rights "atone for [Campbell's] crime against this son of his—against society—against God." Only a moral enlightenment within the white man will suffice.

Chesnutt outlines the nature and effect of this kind of experience in describing the sheriff's agonized pondering over the appearance of this long-forgotten son of his youth. Foreshadowing the climactic moments of truth experienced by later morally myopic New South aristocrats in Chesnutt's fiction, Campbell's "moral faculty," for so long "warped by his environment," undergoes "a kind of clarifying." "Obscuring passions and prejudices" fade away for a moment and all his actions "stand out, in the clear light of truth, in their correct proportions and relations." At this second climactic moment in the story the sheriff finally sees "that he had owed some duty to this son of his,—that neither law nor custom could destroy a responsibility inherent in the nature of mankind." Through the eyes of a progenitor he remembers that he saw "in this mulatto what he himself might have become had not the safeguards of parental restraint and public opinion been thrown around him." Having recognized his hypocrisy beneath his progressive social exterior, the sheriff begins to feel "a great pity" instead of resentment toward his victimized son's desperate condition. He approaches the future unsure of what to do for his son, but with a new sensitivity toward his filial relationship, social obligation, and moral responsibility to the Afro-American.

Within "The Sheriff's Children" lies the germ of practically all Chesnutt's major protest fiction. The seeds of naturalism, melodrama, and sensationalism which sprout from the muck raked up in his late race problem stories and novels are virtually all present in "The Sheriff's Children." But they still do not supplant the basically moral preoccupation which is the hallmark of Chesnutt's literary approach to "the problem." In such experimental stories as "The Bouquet" or "The Web of Circumstance," Chesnutt adapted himself to popular literary modes and employed them with relative success. But most often the themes, structural elements, and plot devices of his problem fiction were patterned on his own literary model, "The Sheriff's Children." The moral consequence of miscegenation, the confrontation of aspiring New Negro and entrenched southern aristocracy, the struggle for social justice in the small-town New South—these are the problems which Chesnutt continued to brood over and to write about with increasing frequency after the republication of "The Sheriff's Children" in *The Wife of His Youth*. The same technical approaches to the exposition of his literary case—the use of revised character types often in atypical roles, the focusing of the action on dramatized discussions of the problem and on melodramatic climaxes of individual moral decision—would reappear after "The Sheriff's Children" in Chesnutt's best-known problem novels. Even the final mood of unrelieved tension in "The Sheriff's Children," originating from conflicting moral demands and private desires impossible fully to resolve or ignore, would become the concluding note of much of the author's most characteristic problem fiction. Thus for the first time in "The Sheriff's Children," Chesnutt combined the two predominant purposes of his color line fiction, analysis and exposure of the caste system in the small-town South together with a sympathetic portrayal of the mulatto as the human product and victim of that unjust system.

Notes

1. "The Bouquet" was first published in the *Atlantic Monthly* 84 (1899): 648–54. It was reprinted in *The Wife of His Youth*, 269–90.

2. See "Fact and Fiction" in the Wilmington (N.C.) *Messenger*, January 28, 1900.

3. William Dean Howells, "Mr. Charles W. Chesnutt's Stories," *Atlantic Monthly* 85 (1900): 700.

4. First published in the New York *Independent*, November 7, 1889, "The Sheriff's Children" was reprinted in *The Wife of His Youth*.

Houston A. Baker Jr.

The first edition of *The Conjure Woman*, Chesnutt's 1899 collection of short stories, immediately reveals what might be called the graphics of minstrelsy. On the cover, a venerably comic black man who is bald and possessed of big ears, rough features, and a great deal of woolly white hair merges—not unintentionally—with two rather malevolent looking caricatures of rabbits. The Houghton, Mifflin and Company designers outdid themselves in suggesting the link between Chesnutt's content and that of the ever popular Joel Chandler Harris's "Uncle Remus" and the crafty Brer Rabbit of Afro-American folk ancestry. There is, to be sure, justification for regarding Chesnutt's work as an expressive instance of the traditional trickster rabbit tales of black folklore, since his main character Uncle Julius manages to acquire gains by strategies that are familiar to students of Brer Rabbit. The real force of *The Conjure Woman*, however, does not reside in a febrile replay of an old Harris tune. Rather, the collection's strength lies in the deep and intensive recoding of form that marks its stories. The work is best characterized as a drama of transformation.

In a letter from Chesnutt to Walter Hines Page in 1898 we find the following:

> Speaking of dialect, it is almost a despairing task to write it.... The fact is, of course, that there is no such thing as a Negro dialect; that what we call by that name is the attempt to express, with such a degree of phonetic correctness as to suggest *the sound*, English pronounced as an ignorant old southern Negro would be supposed to speak it.[1] (Emphasis added)

In these reflections shared with one of the most influential literary editors and brokers of his era, Chesnutt shrewdly gives and takes in a single, long breath. He unequivocally states that the task of the spokesperson who would render black life adequately is to "suggest the *sound.*" At the same time, he knows to whom he is speaking and promptly gives Page something for his fancy—"an ignorant old southern Negro." In a phrase, then, we have encoded the injunction from Chesnutt to *heed the sound* and a disclaimer to Page that says there is no need—really, boss— to fear the sound: it is still that of an ignorant old darky.

Nothing, of course, could be farther from the truth. Chesnutt had been aware for years that the plantation tradition in American letters and even more studied efforts by white authors to write about the Afro-American were inadequate and frequently idiotic. He had also been fully aware that what editors like Page passed off as "Negro life in story" was radically opposed to the story he wanted to tell. Listen again as Chesnutt gives and takes in a single breath.

Having been dithyrambic about the March 1899 issue of *Atlantic* in a letter to Page, he then says, "The dialect story is one of the sort of Southern stories that make me feel it is *my duty* to write a different sort, and yet I did not lay it down without a tear of genuine emotion" (p. 107, my emphasis). As an Afro-American spokesperson, Chesnutt was acutely aware of "his duty" to preserve fidelity to the *sound* of African ancestors and the phonics of their descendants in the "country districts." Rather than producing a simpleminded set of trickster stories framed by the ponderous pretensions of a white Ohio Buckeye as narrator, therefore, he offered a world of sounds and sweet airs that resonates with the transformative power of *conjure.*

Conjure is the transatlantic religion of diasporic and Afro-American masses in the New World. Descended from *vodun,* an African religion in which the priestess holds supreme power, conjure's name in Haiti and the Caribbean is *voodoo.* The force that transmutes and transforms in Chesnutt's volume of stories is the *root work* and empowering mediations of *The Spirit* that mark the efforts of voodoo's Houngans or conjure's "two-headed doctors." In stories of *The Conjure Woman,* we find a struggle in progress as the white, Ohio narrator who has moved to southern "country districts" strives to provide empirical explanations—a certain species of philosophical "nonsense"—as a reassuring mask for the myriad manifestations of Uncle Julius's "spirit work." The seemingly comic old "uncle," in turn, ceaselessly transmits sounds about a cruel order of bondage that has transformed African harmony, as idealized and serene as a Dan mask, into family separation, floggings, and commercial negotiations. But even as Julius relays his sound, he introduces, valorizes, and validates a *root* phonics that is vastly different from the sounds of the Ohio narrator. The *difference* is conjure. For conjure is a power of transformation that causes definitions of "form" as fixed and comprehensible "thing" to dissolve. Black men, considered by slavery as "things" or "chattel personal," are transformed through conjure into seasonal vegetation figures, or trees, or gray wolves. White men, in turn, are transmuted into surly and abused "noo niggers." A black child is changed into a hummingbird and a mockingbird. A black woman becomes a cat, and an elderly black man's clubfoot is a reminder of his transformation—under a conjurer's "revenge"—into a mule.

The fluidity of *The Conjure Woman*'s world, symbolized by such metamorphoses, is a function of the black narrator's mastery of form. The old man knows the sounds that are dear to the hearts of his white boss and his wife, and he presents them with conjuring efficaciousness. In effect, he presents a world in which "dialect" masks the drama of African spirituality challenging and changing the disastrous transformations of slavery. A continuation of this historic masking ritual is at work in the "present" universe of *The Conjure Woman* (the space/time in which Julius relates his stories to Ohioans). For throughout all of the volume's stories the *sound* of African ancestry operates at a low, signifying, and effective register *behind* the mask of a narrational dialect that, in Chesnutt's words, is "no ... thing." Finally, what is sharply modified by the transformative soundings of the work are the dynamics of lordship and bondage as a whole. When the work concludes, Julius has obtained a job, use of a building on the Ohioan's property for black community organizational purposes, employment for his grandson, and (possibly) profits from a duplicitous horse trade. In a sense, one might say that Julius has secured—in the very heart of the country districts—an enclave in which a venerable Afro-American spirit can sound off. During all of the black narrator's tellings, the white Ohioan believes the stories are merely expressive of a minstrel type. He views Julius as, at best, a useful entertainment, one who can do odd jobs *and* tell stories. He considers him, at worst, an agent of annoyance and craftiness—never as a potent force of African transformations that can not be comprehended or controlled by Western philosophy.

But what is meant here by Western philosophy? The Ohioan's reading at the beginning of "The Gray Wolf's Ha'nt" provides an indication of the kind of rational control the white man seeks in the face of formal transmutations. He reads the following passage to his wife "with pleasure":

"The difficulty of dealing with transformations so many-sided as those which all existences have undergone or are undergoing, is such as to make a complete and deductive interpretation almost hopeless. So to grasp the total process of redistribution of matter and motion as to see simultaneously its several necessary results in their actual independence is scarcely possible. There is, however, a mode of rendering the process as a whole tolerably comprehensible."[2]

"John," says his wife, "I wish you would stop reading that *nonsense* and see who that is coming up the lane" (p. 164, my emphasis). Indeed, the process of "redistribution" suggested in the passage is philosophically incomprehensible in Western terms, especially if that very redistribution is being effected from behind the minstrel mask—with the sound of minstrelsy seeming to dominate—by an African sensibility. The transformations wrought in and by Julius's tales are *conjure changes* necessitated by a bizarre economics of slavery. Only spiritual transformations of the "slave" self as well as the "master" self ("Mars Jeems's Nightmare") in a universe governed by *root work* (a work that demands that adherents pay in full to the priestess Aunt Peggy) will enable the progress and survival of a genuinely Afro-American *sound.*

Julius's voice is in fact a function of conjure and a conjuring function. It allows Chesnutt—who, like Julius, is a North Carolinian who has heard "de tale fer twenty-five years ... and ain't got no 'casion for ter 'spute it"—to *sound* a common tale of Afro-American transformative resourcefulness under the guise of an ole "uncle" speaking *nonsense.* The power of Julius and Chesnutt resides in the change they work on their audiences. They put, so to speak, their white hearers through changes. Listen to the Ohioan's wife at the conclusion of "The Conjurer's Revenge"—the tale that appears in advance of the one in which her husband attempts to read "transformation." At the story's close, she condemns Julius's narration as follows: "That story does not appeal to me, Uncle Julius, and is not up to your usual mark.... In fact, it seems to me like nonsense" (p. 127). When the next story opens—"Sis' Becky's Pickaninny"—the mistress has fallen morosely ill and neither "novels" read by John, nor "plantation songs" sung by "the hands" can effect a cure.

In comes Uncle Julius with his *conjure,* and when his tale of Sis' Becky is done—a tale whose moral the wife is able to supply, bringing her and the teller into expressive accord—she begins to improve. *Conjure* is also known, of course, as folk medicine. "My wife's condition," says the Ohioan, "took a turn for the better from this very day, and she was soon on the way to ultimate recovery" (p. 160). Can it come as a surprise that the wife's characterization of two opposed *phonics*—Western philosophical rationalism meant to comprehend and control fluidity, and African conjure meant to move the spirit through a fluid repertoire of "forms"— grants the nod to *conjure?* The designation *nonsense* falls with a heavy thump upon rationalism's polysyllables at the commencement of "The Gray Wolf's Ha'nt." And we know by this token that Julius (like his creator) has played a mojo hand with the deft brilliance of a master of form.

What moves through Chesnutt's collection is the sound of a southern black culture that knew it had to *re-form* a slave world created by the West's willful transformation of Africans into chattel. Conjure's spirit work moves behind—within, and through—the mask of minstrelsy to ensure survival, to operate changes, to acquire necessary resources for continuance, and to cure a sick world. At the first appearance of Chesnutt's "conjure" stories in the *Atlantic* (and in his correspondence, the word "conjure" is always in quotes, protected as a *tricky* or transformative sign—masked), a white audience thought they were hearing merely entertaining syllables of a lovable darky. The turn-of-the-century writer's goal, however, was a "different story" for a different world, and he achieved this black southern eloquence in a discourse unequaled in his day.

Notes

1. Helen M. Chesnutt, *Charles Waddell Chesnutt: Pioneer of the Color Line* (Chapel Hill: U of North Carolina P, 1952) 241. All further references to Chesnutt's correspondence, marked by page numbers in parentheses, are to this volume.

2. Charles Waddell Chesnutt, *The Conjure Woman* (1899; rpt. Ann Arbor: U of Michigan P, 1969) 163–64. All subsequent references to Chesnutt's collection are marked by page numbers in parentheses.

Eric J. Sundquist

In 1901 Chesnutt contributed to *Modern Culture* an essay, "Superstitions and Folklore of the South."[1] What is remarkable about it, especially in light of Chesnutt's conjure tales, is his apparent degree of skepticism about black folk beliefs. In charting the background of his Uncle Julius stories, Chesnutt carefully records methods and instances of "conjuration" practiced by purported conjure doctors, both women and men. But the emphasis falls decidedly on the various rational explanations that can be put forward to account for the apparent success of any curse or cure. Old Aunt Harriet, who claims to have extracted a snake from her own arm (inhabitation by reptiles is one of the most common signs of conjure in the folk records of the day), is represented by Chesnutt as "lying" or "merely self-deluded." Her religion is probably little more than "superstition," and her belief that a mystic voice brought her a cure for an ankle sprain appears to be written off by Chesnutt: "She is not the first person to hear spirit voices in his or her own vagrant imaginings." Old Uncle Jim, another informant, is but a "shrewd, hard old sinner, and a palpable fraud." As Chesnutt records it, conjure thrives on "delusion" and the "credulity of ignorance," signaling the "relics of ancestral barbarism" that have not yet been shaken off as African Americans become more civilized. In these animadversions Chesnutt seemed to be little different from the majority of ethnologists and folklorists who had begun in earnest to collect material about conjure at the end of the nineteenth century. The overwhelming reliance on theories of racial hierarchy and the progress of civilization, fueled by the twin engines of science and Christianity, made any response but skepticism unlikely. Most ethnography about conjure (or "hoodoo") stigmatized such elements of slave culture and its aftermath as superstition or delusion—of interest from an anthropological point of view but nonetheless irrational and regressive—and implicitly cooperated with sociological theory and legal proscription to identify the potential for "reversion" and "degeneration" to forms of primitivism among contemporary African Americans who did not aspire to a more assimilated American middle class.

Given his own precarious position straddling the color line, and given his clear aspirations to middle-class professional respectability, it is not surprising that Chesnutt would detach himself from the irrationality of conjure. For this reason alone, his characterizations of conjure would be central to any estimate of his role as a writer committed to the notice and preservation of distinct black American traditions at an especially difficult historical moment when the legislated "superstitions" of Jim Crow held full sway. If the conjure tales in particular are evidence of such a commitment, they are nevertheless tales in which Chesnutt's curt personal belief that conjure was "superstition" is marked and in which his own imaginative transformation of the folk material, not its original substance, is predominant. Or so it seems: Chesnutt no doubt identified to some degree with the skepticism voiced in the white narrative frames of his own conjure stories; and yet it is the black liminal voice of the trickster, immersed in the strategies if not the actual secrets of conjure, whose historical memory and cultural values are most at stake in these stories. Chesnutt, that is to say, may himself have been signifying in "Superstitions and Folklore of the South" (the essay's several oblique allusions to the barbarity of segregation and the fetish of race purity are one kind of evidence), adopting the isolating voice of contemporary ethnography while working inside it in order to preserve African American cultural forms and to make them instruments of his own gain, much as his character Uncle Julius does in the tales. Chesnutt, one could say, was doing a literary cakewalk that assumed ever grander and yet more detailed, subtly argued forms over the course of his writing career.

Preservation and transformation exist in a taut balance in the nineteenth-century ethnographic record of black folktales, and Chesnutt's focus on his *literary* appropriation of folk forms exacerbates rather than diminishes that tension. Seeming to remove himself as far as possible from the "original" tales of slave culture, Chesnutt pointed on several occasions to the privilege of authorial license, most notably in his late essay "Post-Bellum—Pre-Harlem," in which he remarked that with one exception his conjure tales were "the fruit of my own imagination, in which respect they differ from the Uncle Remus stories which are avowedly folktales." And other critics have followed his lead in differentiating him from Joel Chandler Harris, who, as Chesnutt put it in the 1901 conjure essay, "with fine literary discrimination collected and put into pleasing and enduring form, the plantation stories which dealt with animals."[2] Chesnutt's relationship with Harris is complex and worthy of extended discussion, which will follow. The difference between them, however, here asserted by Chesnutt on the spurious basis of an opposition between folklore and imagination, is no simple one but must instead be read within the overarching problem of African American cultural origins and African retentions. His account of the origins of his own versions of conjure tales was extremely canny and was dedicated to the promotion of his own career as a writer. But one must begin with the fact, as Robert Hemenway has demonstrated in his landmark essay on Chesnutt's folklore, that there are numerous sources—or, at any rate, analogues—for many of the central features of his conjure tales. This fact alone places Chesnutt in a strikingly complicated relation to the issue of African retentions, for whatever his ultimate assessment of the cultural value of African American folk beliefs in the late nineteenth century, Chesnutt appears to have followed Harris and others in their view that, though many black stories were part of the world's stock of wonder stories, appearing throughout racially distinct cultures or reflecting European origins, some of the tales had specific African beginnings. Although they are related to animal trickster tales and to other story paradigms such as the Master-John cycle, conjure tales were constituted, for Chesnutt, by a relatively distinct body of imaginative structures that were at once more amenable to narrative transfiguration and more precisely traceable to the ancestry of slave culture. The belief in conjure, he observed, was rooted in "African fetichism, which was brought over from the dark continent." Lacking the "sanctions of religion and custom" that supported them in Africa, such beliefs became, "in the shadow of the white man's civilization, a pale reflection of their former selves."[3]

This "pale reflection" that African beliefs became under the pressure of enslavement and American acculturation corresponds, moreover, to the explanation that Chesnutt offered of his own imaginative processes. Whereas he first thought—or remembered—that only "The Goophered Grapevine" came directly from black folklore, his interviews with elderly blacks, including a conjure man, reminded him that some of his seemingly imaginative innovations were "but dormant ideas, lodged in my childish mind by old Aunt This and old Uncle That, and awaiting only the spur of imagination to bring them again to the surface." Ches-

nutt's eminently Hawthornian account of his creativity—a literary influence that is evident in the tales themselves—puts a limit on the liberty
exercised by the artist: ideas must already exist "somewhere in his consciousness," ready to be subjected to the "power of rearrangement."[4]
Yet Chesnutt's admission (or his recognition, as the case may be) about
the sources of his tales is interesting not for what it takes away from his
artistry but for what it adds. By locating elements of his stories in the
childhood tales told him by elders of the generation of slavery, Chesnutt
placed himself closer to those originating beliefs that had become only
a pale reflection of their former African selves, and he made the remem-
brance of slave culture a foundation for modern African American culture. More pointedly than Harris or other white folklorists, Chesnutt
found himself at a demanding double remove—separated from the generations of slavery as they were in turn separated from all but the most
resilient elements of African culture. But he made of this distance a
powerful instrument to demystify the positivist constructions of pri-
mary material by folklorists, blurring the line between redaction and
creation in a most profound way. The literary category of the imagination, which at first appears to separate Chesnutt's work from the "folktales" of Harris and the conjure beliefs collected by professional ethno-
graphers, circles back, by the path of personal and historical memory, to
merge his narrative art with the stories of the black ancestors. Chesnutt's theory suggests, too, that the distinction between the rearranging
power of the imagination and the bequest of folklore is a tenuous one.
Just as Harris's Br'er Rabbit tales must be seen as the product of the
transforming forces of folk storytelling, long before Harris set them in
his own problematically imagined plantation frames, so Chesnutt's con-
sciously fabricated tales contain materials that were far from stagnant
but instead were structured according to particular cultural pressures
and belief patterns that had evolved generation after generation, from
Africa to the New World, absorbing new European American elements
along the way.

Chesnutt was resolutely middle class, and the majority of his published fiction, especially his color line stories and *The Marrow of Tradition*,
reflects in some measure his genteel literary tastes. At the same time,
however, his fiction also reflects his concern that the rise of a black middle class could jeopardize racial cohesiveness in the very act of uplifting
the race and sacrifice a distinctive strain of African American art whose
record lay in the oral narratives. Leroi Jones (Amiri Baraka) is thus widely
off the mark in his claim that Chesnutt subscribed to the proposition, a

sign of "slave mentality," that the Negro "must completely lose himself within the culture and social order of the ex-master," and counted himself part of that black middle class that "wanted no subculture, nothing that could connect them with the poor black man or the slave."[5] The black middle class often ignored or ridiculed the folk culture that survived in trickster stories and plantation tales, in minstrelsy, and on the black stage, or that was preserved in the spirituals and was beginning to flourish in jazz, but Chesnutt incorporated those folk voices into his writing in the most remarkable ways. Indeed, he made such a rift within African American culture the very subject of his writing because it was, in perfectly visible ways, the subject of his life as a man of mixed race light enough to pass for white. One could say that his exploration of class and color divisions produced in Chesnutt an uneasy adherence to a "subculture" that was part of, not separate from, the middle class; the lower class, the "folk," and the reminders of slavery itself were contained "somewhere in its consciousness," just as the folk beliefs of African origin were contained somewhere in Chesnutt's own imaginative reservoir. The tension between the two realms, and the signs of Chesnutt's honest recognition of his moral obligation to keep them united, appear throughout his fiction. Not the best, perhaps, but the most classic statement is found in his famous story "The Wife of His Youth."

First appearing in the *Atlantic Monthly* in 1898, the story was collected the following year in *The Wife of His Youth and Other Stories of the Color Line.* The plot, of course, concerns the dilemma confronted by a northern, upper-middle-class mulatto, a member of the best "Blue Vein" society of Groveland (modeled on Chesnutt's own Cleveland), when he must decide whether or not to acknowledge the validity of his marriage during slavery to a dark-skinned, illiterate woman from whom he was separated but who reappears on the eve of his engagement to a beautiful light-skinned woman of his own class. The story has a place in the larger structure of concerns examined in the color line stories as a group; but one can notice here several aspects of the story that illuminate Chesnutt's relation to his conjure stories as part of the "subcultural" content that had to be similarly acknowledged in his own career. By her coincidental appearance upon the scene, Ryder's wife, Liza Jane, interrupts his idyllic visions of increased assimilation of European cultural standards and upward progress through a further lightening of his children's dark skin. Standing in stark contrast to his fantasy of a social world represented by Tennyson's poem "A Dream of Fair Women," Liza Jane, who is "very black,—so black that her toothless gums, revealed when she opened her mouth to speak, were not red, but blue," looks "like a bit of the old plantation life, summoned up from the past by the wave of a magician's wand." She is undeterred by the slim chances of finding the husband of her youth and tells Ryder, apparently without knowing yet who he is, that "de signs an' de tokens" have guided her search.[6]

In addition to its role in Chesnutt's critique of color consciousness and intraracial racism, "The Wife of His Youth," written at the same time he was organizing a collection of his conjure stories, represents a meditation upon the complexities of his own acknowledgment of a past—not the literal past of his youth (although that is part of it as well) but rather the symbolic past of his race. Liza Jane seems summoned up as though by conjure, a reminder of Ryder's as well as Chesnutt's obligation to confront and, as Ryder finally does, to embrace a painful past and the culture that is carried with it. The embrace is nothing if not ambivalent. As Alice Walker reminds us, Ryder's black wife is too old to bear children, and his declaration that "our fate lies between absorption by the white race and extinction in the black" (complete with its bitingly ironic allusion to Lincoln: "with malice towards none ...") therefore does not present to him quite the moral dilemma that it appears to. But Ryder's choice operates on other levels as well. Included within his recognition of Liza Jane are several implicit indications of Chesnutt's own cultural obligations: to join with the lower classes in the struggle for rights; to put the good of the community before the advances of the few who are able to enter directly into the white social and cultural mainstream; and to take control of the popular conceptions of "old plantation life" that are being generated by racist commentary and unscrupulous artistry. In an age dominated by literary accounts of sectional reunion symbolized by North-South romantic alliances, Chesnutt's stories of reunion were typically dedicated to the postbellum reunification of scattered or racially divided black families. Marriage was a sign of communal healing, just as it remained, in the color line plots, a sign of continuing racism. In either case it was for Chesnutt also a metaphor for his art and for his place within an American literary community that was at best only tolerant of, and usually antagonistic toward, any but the mildest portraits of racial conflict. When Ryder narrates the story of his wife to the gathered throng of his middle-class peers, he speaks "in the same soft dialect, which came readily to his lips," that his wife had used earlier. What they hear in his story and in his voice are those "wrongs and sufferings of this past generation" that they usually ignore but that all of them "still felt, in their darker moments," as a "shadow hanging over them."[7]

Werner Sollors has suggested that "The Wife of His Youth" is a story in which the conflict between cultural "consent" (choice of a culture defined outside inherited ethnic or racial boundaries) and cultural "descent" (acceptance of inherited categories based on race) is marked. One must add to this that it is not Ryder alone who is the storyteller here but Chesnutt too. Like Ryder, he speaks in a dialect that is not his own but that comes readily to his lips, and in doing so he instantly casts in a critical light the post-Reconstruction vogue of dialect plantation literature by authors such as Thomas Nelson Page and Joel Chandler Harris, who wrote from the other side of the color line.[8] Chesnutt's pun on "darker" is a reminder that color is a fluid category, a mask that can hide but cannot obliterate a cultural past—and a mask that, as the rise of "one-drop" segregation made evident, could easily be punctured. The story self-consciously adopts a kind of mask, however, for although we are told Ryder reproduces Liza Jane's dialect in retelling her story, the text itself does not do so. One of the era's favorite literary devices and a necessary focal point for any interpretation of Chesnutt's relation to race writing at the turn of the century, dialect remains a sign of difference, a part of the past that Ryder accepts, even imitates, but that Chesnutt does not actually reproduce. It is a sign, that is to say, of Chesnutt's own very subtle acknowledgment of his complex "blackness" alongside his own membership in the best mulatto society. Liza Jane, a bit of the old plantation conjured up in his middle-class imagination, speaks in an alien voice, but one that Chesnutt knows to be bound indissolubly to his own cultural life. "The Wife of His Youth," then, may be read in part as an emblem of Chesnutt's divided sensibilities. His recognition of his own "wife" lay in the tribute his first book of stories, *The Conjure Woman,* paid to a world that was at once hindered by degradation and ignorance according to the standards of white middle-class society, but at the same time alive with powerful knowledge and cultural meaning generated on hidden but distinguishable African American planes of discourse.

Notes

1. Charles W. Chesnutt, "Superstition and Folklore of the South," *Modern Culture* 13 (1901): 231–35; rpt. in Alan Dundes, ed., *Mother Wit from the*

Laughing Barrel: Readings in the Interpretation of Afro-American Folklore (1973; rpt. New York: Garland, 1981) 369–76.

2. Chesnutt, "Post-Bellum—Pre-Harlem," *Crisis* (1931); rpt. in *Breaking into Print*, ed. Elmer Adler (1937; rpt. Freeport, N.Y., Books for Libraries, 1968) 50; Chesnutt, "Superstition and Folklore of the South," 371.

3. Robert Hemenway, "The Functions of Folklore in Charles Chesnutt's *The Conjure Woman*," *Journal of the Folklore Institute* 13 (1976): 283–309; Chesnutt, "Superstition and Folklore of the South," 371.

4. Chesnutt, "Superstition and Folklore of the South," 372.

5. Leroi Jones [Amiri Baraka], *Blues People: Negro Music in White America* (New York: William Morrow, 1963) 58–9, 131–2.

6. Chesnutt, *The Wife of His Youth and Other Stories* (Ann Arbor: U of Michigan P, 1968) 8–10, 14.

7. Alice Walker, *In Search of Our Mother's Gardens* (New York: Harcourt Brace Jovanovich) 300; Chesnutt, *The Wife of His Youth*, 7, 20.

8. Werner Sollors, *Beyond Ethnicity: Consent and Descent in American Culture* (New York: Oxford UP, 1986) 160–66; William L. Andrews, *The Literary Career of Charles W. Chesnutt* (Baton Rouge: Louisiana State UP, 1980) 39–73.

Ben Slote

Like a lot of young academics who came to their interest in American literature through canonical routes, I first studied Charles Chesnutt's writing in the mid-1980s by reading *The Conjure Woman* and teaching "The Goophered Grapevine." I have since discovered the distortions that attend this introduction when it, like any other, is made to stand for even so brief a literary career. Yet, from trying to teach the story a half dozen times in survey courses, reading some of the ingenious historical and poststructuralist criticism on *The Conjure Woman,* and dwelling in the yawning gulf between those two experiences, I have also discovered something deeply appropriate about coming to Chesnutt where and when I did. If "The Goophered Grapevine" is about its own complacent reception, as a number of critics have suggested, teaching it suggests that the same sort of reception is one for which many of my culturally mainstream students seem historically well equipped. The story acts as a kind of lens under which cultural parallels between post-Reconstruction and Reagan-Bush America emerge. Its self-consciousness is responsive to an unself-consciousness about race politics that characterizes both eras.

This becomes vividly apparent when one compares the race iconography in "The Goophered Grapevine" to the iconography in those recently popular TV commercials for California raisins, first run in the mid-1980s, in which claymation raisin figures with negroid features sing and dance to the Marvin Gaye song "I Heard It through the Grapevine." The deconstructive energies of Chesnutt's story become clarified if one applies them to the commercials' conjurings. More surprisingly, though, "The Goophered Grapevine" 's "subversiveness," which both predicts and accommodates the popularity of *The Conjure Woman* stories, indulges the very kind of obliviousness that the commercials exploit. Reading backwards from the commercials to the story thus also helps explain the

Originally published as "Listening to 'The Goophered Grapevine' and Hearing Raisins Sing," *American Literary History* 6 (Winter 1994): 684–94. Reprinted by permission of Oxford University Press.

143

political limitations of Chesnutt's dialect fiction—in Chesnutt's career and in many of our current classrooms, something which poststructuralist interpretations may obscure.

On the surface, all that seems to justify my comparison *are* surfaces. In Julius's story, told within John's narrative frame, a black man is changed so that his head looks "des like a bunch er grapes."[1] In the commercials, dried grapes are also converted into human heads (with stemlike appendages), and the heads are identifiable as African American; in later commercials this identification becomes quite precise: a "Michael Jackson" raisin spinning with one silver glove, a "Jimi Hendrix" raisin playing left-handed guitar and wearing a headband, a "Ray Charles" raisin with Ray Charles sunglasses, et cetera (for the Ray Charles figure the creators of the commercials "first spent 45 minutes shooting reference film of the real Ray Charles."[2]

The grape connection between the tale and the commercials is mostly, though, a fortuitous coincidence that signals deeper parallels, ones that arise when we consider the motives and results of these transformations. In the story, Henry the slave is transformed because of his master's desire for profit. We recall that McAdoo, the plantation owner, commissions the original goophering of the vineyard to deter slaves from eating the grapes gratis, right off the vine. It works. After McAdoo invests $10 with Aunt Peggy the conjure woman, the fearful slaves lay off and McAdoo realizes what he calls (in Julius's rendition) the "monst'us good intrus" of 1,500 gallons of wine a year (18). When the newly purchased Henry eats the grapes, not knowing of the hex, the overseer has the conjure woman preserve Henry, the newest investment, with another goopher. The result of this remedy, the seasonal fluctuations in Henry's strength, is what generates even more profits for McAdoo. He makes $1,000 a year by selling Henry high in his robust spring health and buying him back cheap in his autumnal decrepitude. In our modern video fable, the commissioners of reification, the California Raisin Advisory Board, and the California raisin growers and packers the board represents are animated by the same motives and have enjoyed the same results.[3] Stage one: the swift rise in crop profits, resulting from what advertisers call the elevation of image—says Clyde Nef, manager of the raisin board, "people" no longer "[think] of raisins as dull, wimpy uninteresting little dark things"—and these profits are not eroded by high overhead; as Nef jokes, "we don't have to pay the stars [the motown raisins] royalties."[4] Stage two: the generation, by 1988, of huge secondary profits from 500 million dollars worth of spin-off merchandizing—"bedsheets, T-shirts, lunch pails, backpacks, toys and about 300 other products" (Barrier 57), none of which goes to the claymation creators, for now our modern equivalents of Aunt Peggy, the conjure woman.

Most suggestive, though, is how similarly the two forms of entertainment are consumed, at least at one level. By the way he listens and responds to Julius's tale, John defines it the way most of Chesnutt's first readers did, as nonserious entertainment, in the words of an 1899 review in the St. Paul *Dispatch*, as a "relief from the serious fiction of the day."[5] Which is to say that the story at least accommodates the same sort of blindness to political figuration that the commercials require: both performances can be exclusively entertaining only of course if one does not recognize that the transformation of people into consumable, edible things describes—nearly literalizes—the dehumanizing economic logic of race oppression. (In the commercials it could only be clearer if the raisins looked like migrant workers.) Remarkably, America does not wince at the motown raisins' minstrelsy, does not come close to recognizing in the race iconography a negrophobia that, as Berndt Ostendorf has noted, always lies beneath the negrophilia of blackface.[6] America has instead done what John the narrator did: eaten it up.

Happily, as critics have for some time noticed, Chesnutt's story is much more self-conscious about its own consumption than its narrator is. John's consuming after the inner tale, his perfunctory purchase of both the vineyard and Uncle Julius's labor, is only the last of many signals that subvert, by collectively thematizing, a complacent, nonserious reading of Julius's story. Indeed, in ways that recent poststructuralist criticism helps make available, it is not hard to see how Chesnutt's story predicts the same consumer dynamics that the commercials construct. Most obviously this is accomplished by the marginal, figurative reading of the tale that Annie, John's wife, represents. When Julius finishes his story, she asks, "doubtfully, but seriously," whether it is true (33). By raising, through Annie, the possibility that Julius's story of fantastic transformations contains some truth, Chesnutt also raises the possibility that this truth is one that John and the complacent reader of plantation fiction actively, if unconsciously, resist. Furthermore, the source of John's condescending skepticism suggests that his resistance to Julius's seriousness is highly self-interested. John does not believe Julius because John is a man of empirical sureness—he likes to act in what he calls "the coolness of judgment" (4)—and because Julius's apparent narrative destination, that some of the old McAdoo grapes are still goo-phered, is for John "doubtless ... accounted for" by the "respectable revenue" that Julius has been making from the wild vineyard before John and Annie come down from the North (35). By the logic of posi-tivistic self-interest, then, John reads Julius's story as narrowly as the post-Reconstruction North reads the history of the South and surely as narrowly as most white TV viewers process the race iconography of the raisin commercials—that is, narrowly enough to preserve their invest-ment in their own appetites. John's final assumption, that the coachman wages he will pay Julius are "more than an equivalent for anything he lost by the sale of the vineyard" (35), only makes the convenience of this system of values obvious. Without the burden of any enlarged sense of expense, John can buy the vineyard and convert it into what the "local press" calls " a striking illustration of the opportunities open to Northern capital in the development of Southern industries" (34)— exactly the sort of arrangement that motivated Federal permissiveness toward the Jim Crow South and underlay such legislative revisions as the 1875 repeal of the Civil Rights Act and the Hayes-Tilden Compro-mise of 1877. Similarly, the conversion of African-American musicians into consumable mascots becomes particularly tolerable when the inconvenience of affirmative action and civil rights legislation is being rigorously rediscovered.

Yet, as Craig Werner suggests in his Derridian and Gatesian reading of *The Conjure Woman*, John here assumes the role of the lion, while Julius and his creator assume that of the signifyin(g) monkey, capitalizing on the preconceptions by which lions, Northern post-Reconstruction capi-talists, and genteel readers of plantation fiction read and construct racial identity. For Werner, Julius's acts of self-interest performed throughout *The Conjure Woman* constitute "transparent economic mask[s]" (353), a kind of blackface that gratifies John's "Euro-Ameri-can oppositional" way of thinking (351). The disguise is reinforced by Julius's performances of what Eric Selinger calls "minstrelized 'gusto' " —Julius's own relish of the grapes at the beginning (which John him-self calls a "performance" though he assumes Julius does not know he and Annie see him) and Julius's characterization of the lip-smackin', eye-rollin' affection for scuppernong grapes that all negroes hold.[7] For Werner, this outward countenance of Julius's disguises what is behind his real face. By repeatedly showing John what he wants to see and believe, Julius is able to maintain "control ... over the context in which he can direct his 'marginal' address to Annie to communal rather than individual benefits" (354). And the commercials? This kind of surreptitiously expanded context and its attendant decentering of naturalizing, sense-making constructs is of course exactly the kind of consciousness that the raisin commercials—like any advertisement—cannot afford.

The racist construction that the commercials require of their viewers is perhaps even more clearly described by the way John first listens to Julius's tale. John tells us that "[a]t first the current of his [Julius's] memory—or imagination—seemed somewhat sluggish; but as his embarrassment wore off, his language flowed more freely, and the story acquired perspective and coherence. As he became more and more absorbed in the narrative, his eyes assumed a dreamy expression, and he seemed to lose sight of his auditors, and to be living over again in monologue his life on the old plantation" (12). Given that Julius's tale keeps its auditors entirely *in* his "sight," given that its deconstruction of binarisms of history (ante- and postbellum) and geography (South and North) makes the tale about *new* "plantations" too, and given that Julius's subversive signifyin(g) undoes the racial binarism tied to his so-called "embarrassment" before white auditors, this description of reception rather brilliantly invites a deconstruction of the "perspective and coherence" it seeks to impose. By projecting onto Julius's discourse a sense-making boundary or context, John dramatizes both what Jonathan Culler calls "the infinite extendability of context" and his own implication in a context quite close to Julius's immediate reference.[8] The commercials invite no such expansion. They do not self-consciously describe and mediate the product's consumption; they seek to cut out the middle man and instead simulate, through their apparent mimetic loyalty, especially their apparent three-dimensionality, a real, palpable, edible reality. (If Chesnutt's story is in some way writerly, the commercials are in all ways "readerly"—or, if you will, eaterly.) These are raisins singing, not people singing and pretending to be raisins. Thus the commercials collapse the difference between person and thing only to widen the hierarchical racial binarism they exploit: Marvin Gaye, Ray Charles, even Michael Jackson, have become the "little dark things" of the consuming viewer.

When juxtaposed to the singleness of the commercials' purpose, the subversive play of Chesnutt's dialect stories emerges quite clearly, I think. And yet, if we expand our sense of the story's energies beyond its immediate narrative boundaries, we must see, too, that the consumer dynamics that animate the commercials' reifications also suggest the political limitations of Chesnutt's play. If one can say that, through John, Chesnutt predicts and even indicts a reader's trivialization of post-Reconstruction African-American experience, one cannot say that his dialect stories prevent this trivialization or even that they seek to prevent it. Indeed, with our raisins in mind, the consumption of racial iconography described by "The Goophered Grapevine" also seems to gratify—or predict as unpreventable—the entertained, complacent reception his conjure stories did in fact receive. Although John's molding of Julius's story appears to us conspicuously self-serving, Chesnutt's molding of the whole story, like his eventual construction of *The Conjure Woman*, ends up serving the same exploitative purpose. In this way, the closest equivalent to our claymation creators, conjuring on behalf of the owners of the fields, is not Aunt Peggy but Chesnutt himself.

Chesnutt was predictably self-conscious about *The Conjure Woman*'s cultural and political design. In his 1931 essay, "Post-Bellum—Pre-Harlem," he was, as William Andrews puts it, quick to "insist that [the stories] were *artistic* creations, not folkloric transcriptions," distancing himself from Joel Chandler Harris (45). (The formal similarities between *The Conjure Woman* stories and those of *Uncle Remus* are precise enough for Werner to argue that Chesnutt is deconstructing Harris.) Yet after writing only three such stories, Chesnutt's artistic ambitions had convinced him to move beyond conjure stories altogether—that is, until Walter Hines Page, editor of the *Atlantic Monthly* and senior member of Houghton Mifflin, suggested that a book of such stories of black superstition was marketable (Andrews 31). In his late essay, Chesnutt asserted that, aside from "The Goophered Grapevine," all *The Conjure Woman* stories were "the fruit of my own imagination."[9] Seizing his half-considered metaphor is not completely unfair when one recalls whose tastes his "fruit" fed. When, in 1898, Chesnutt was arranging the order of stories in *The Conjure Woman*, he decided to put "Hot-Foot Hannibal" last because, he said, it leaves "a good taste in the mouth."[10] In that story, Julius's tale telling ends up uniting two young white lovers, Annie's Yankee sister and Malcolm Murchison, a gallant Southerner. Thus it both identifies, with allegorical precision, and gratifies the very sort of narrative desires that sustain and are sustained by plantation fiction. Certainly that is the "good taste." The bad taste, detectable in Julius's inner story about the fatal jealousies of enslaved black lovers, is one that Chesnutt presumably hoped most readers did not detect or were "relieved of" by the end of John's narration. With our raisins in mind, the "relief" detected by contemporary reviewers of *The Conjure Woman* should recall for us Fredric Jameson's sense of the political role of pop-cultural discourse—its raising of cultural mainstream fears in order to safely discharge them.

And what of the tale that was not the fruit of Chesnutt's imagination? If the expansive figurative energy of "The Goophered Grapevine" raises the specter of democratic anxiety, surely the story equips the reader to discharge that anxiety by blithefully equating, at the end, Julius's new post-Reconstruction employment with his old Reconstruction ownership and by inviting all along an incredulous white reception of its "charming" superstitions. Such may be the inevitable consequences of bringing one culture's fruit to another culture's table. When Chesnutt took the African-American folktale from the lips of his father-in-law's black gardener, remolded it, and placed it in the pages of the *Atlantic Monthly*, he not only broke into the belletristic forum he so ardently desired but also, as they say in the record industry, "crossed over." Given how historically late Chesnutt's use of the plantation genre was, our best pop-music analogy might not be '60s motown music, with its unprecedented crossover popularity, but the '80s motown revival, which pushed that music almost entirely beyond cultural liminality, not so much cross-over as just *over.* (It is useful to recall the movie vehicle for the motown revival, *The Big Chill* [1983].) Our raisins may be the inevitable result of such momentum. Cornel West has described Marvin Gaye as a popular artist who has helped keep West "alive."[11] If this is still the case for him or for any African American, the commercials at least dramatize the difficulties in preserving such vitality.

By my comparison I have to meant to suggest that "The Goophered Grapevine" constitutes Chesnutt's attempt at literary passing or that in *The Conjure Woman* he acts in what Forrest Robinson calls, in a different context, literary "bad faith," gratifying his readers' moral complacency while seeming to criticize it. Instead, through the commercials, I finally mean to express a worry, that the modern critical ingenuity that his stories so wonderfully reward can replace some practical sense of the politics of their consumption. From my experience and the experience of a number of colleagues, this worry needs to be applied to the "American lit." survey classroom, where literary snacking is always at risk and where "The Goophered Grapevine" is still often the only Chesnutt on the menu (it is the one piece of his in the latest edition of the Norton anthology). The afterlife of the story's iconography should suggest the need to make our students self-conscious about its accommodating appearance and our institutional acceptance of its particular invitation—

which is more self-consciousness than one 50 minute class can usually raise. Worse, there is the dangerous irony that some students may leave their sampling of Chesnutt more complacent or John-like as readers than they were before. Pamela Caughie describes a similarly reticent, self-protective interpretive posture in her white students when they discuss Nella Larsen's *Passing* and wisely suggests that such reticences have become a kind of occupational hazard in multicultural classrooms.[12]

Short of the kind of indicting harangue that calcifies reticence, how does one prevent such thin, self-protective responses? Is there really a way to have a student centered discussion in, say, a class of nonmajors that authentically discovers the decentering habits of Chesnutt's fiction? More generally, at the intersection of multiculturalism and poststructuralism, how exactly might we proceed pedagogically? It is well and good to raise worries about the politics of misinference—or the politics of an autocratic pedagogy—but what actually might one *do* with these worries in the classroom? As with most articles of this kind (including Caughie's important one), mine is unfortunately longer on worries than concrete responses. Still, let me conclude with two remedial choices, neither sufficient—with many students something like a pedagogical goopher seems in order—but both practicable.

If one is institutionally obliged to represent Chesnutt with one work, consider a different text, *The Marrow of Tradition* (1901), where the author's political aggression, while still deft, is less avoidable. There the "claymation" is more clearly deconstructive. For example, in a scene before the first would-be climax of that book, old Mr. Delamere argues that his loyal black attendant could not have committed the robbery and murder he is accused of (and may soon be lynched for) because the servant " 'has too much respect for the [Delamere] family to do anything that would reflect disgrace upon it.... A white family raised him. Like all the negroes, he has been clay in the hands of the white people. They are what we have made them or permitted them to become.' "[13] Another fortuitous metaphor for us, yet the contextual irony it sustains is typical of the novel. The good Delamere means to be self-incriminating by his race-as-clay trope, yet the figure undoes his argument and in the process reminds us of the conspicuous frailty of, and lethal contradictions in, white intentions or white-handed manipulations in the novel. (The servant is framed by Delamere's own grandson and another servant is murdered by a white mob precisely because both servants act out their pliant devotion to white training.) Rhetorically, Delamere's clay trope has the double problem of helping him explore the logic of culpability in order to plead innocence and of resting it all on the logic of noblesse oblige and the naturalized moral value of family names, which the action of the book has, by this point, totally undermined. These ironies anticipate larger, dramatic ones. The reader soon finds out that the old man's good name cannot get his servant out of jail without the help of arbitrarily revealed circumstances; and when his name and his hand conspire to work their final act of goodness, that is, the revising of his will so that Dr. Miller's "colored hospital" receives most of his old fortune (and his degenerate grandson none at all), history and other conspiracies foil him altogether. Delamere's will is suppressed, undone, like another kindly patriarch's will in the novel and like almost all the highly flourished intentions, good and bad, in the book. In the novel's real climax, the colored hospital burns to the ground.

The novel's political energy may be less avoidable for students than that of *The Conjure Woman* tales because that energy is narratological, not iconographic. Alongside what John Wideman calls its "variety of narrative modes," *The Marrow of Tradition* creates a variety of unfulfilled narrative expectations through the good and evil plotting of certain characters but also through its own proximity to various narrative genres: the "tragic mulatto" story, post-Reconstruction plantation melodrama, domestic romance, historical fiction (with the Wilmington riot plainly in the background), and African-American folklore.[14] Despite what we expect, old Delamere's aristocratic plea neither succeeds nor fails; his servant is not lynched, and this fact neither prevents nor precipitates the race riot we have been expecting for most of the book but do not get for seven more chapters. Conventional narrative trajectories within the book, like the conventional assumptions of authority that generate them, are continually deflected by the writerly authority outside it. In the terms of our creation trope, Chesnutt rigorously molds his raw historical and literary material only to unmold it; he works with hands whose manipulations seem familiar but always prove conspicuously, aggressively alien, hands of no known color.

Another way past irresponsible consumption may be to have the students get at "The Goophered Grapevine" in highly contextualized ways. If historicizing the story's reception and its place in Chesnutt's career takes more time than one has, one might at least read it alongside other writings from the African-American vineyard, including Langston Hughes's deferred dream, drying like a raisin in the sun—and exploding—or Jean Toomer's short poem "Face":

> Hair—
> silver-gray,
> like streams of stars,
> Brows—
> recurved canoes
> quivered by the ripples blown by pain,
> Her eyes—
> mist of tears
> condensing on the flesh below
> And her channeled muscles
> are cluster grapes of sorrow
> purple in the evening sun
> nearly ripe for worms.[15]

At which point, with the consumability of images of race thus prob-
lematized, students might indeed be ripe for the critical viewing of a
raisin commercial. Their greater responsiveness to visual media (long a
complaint in literature departments) could here help take them toward
a self-consciousness about cultural consumption that brings large
rewards. Most obviously but most ideally, in a time when responses to
cultural oppression have (with TV's help) become stylized or displaced
into personal sentiment, students would be equipped to recognize the
operation of ideology, including racist ideology, in our economy and
mainstream culture, the sort of extrapersonal vision that might complicate their consumption of all discourses, not just those with conspicuous sponsorship. By juxtaposing the commercial and Chesnutt's story
and by comparing their responses to each, students would also be learning how to extend to the literary field the constructive impulses by
which many of them already know to suspect the truth claims of adver-
tisements. A good many students who have not or cannot read poststructuralist criticism are wise to the totalizing binarism by which the
Coke/Pepsi "choice" (or any product choice) seeks to erase competi-
tion. It is a short step from here to their recognizing a politics of exclusion and gaining a practical understanding of how well multicultural
practices articulate poststructuralist thinking.

At the very least, a class that combined "The Goophered Grapevine"
with a California raisin commercial and takes up the kind of possibilities
for intertextual interpretations explored here seems sure to get at more
of the story's ingenuity and political sinew than many students are get-
ting now. Careful with this "remedy," though. We need to remember, as

teachers and as interpreters, what Chesnutt found out after *The Conjure Woman*: you can't get to a political consciousness through the stomach.

Notes

1. Charles W. Chesnutt, *The Conjure Woman* (1899; rpt. Ann Arbor: U of Michigan P, 1969) 22. Future references to this edition appear parenthetically within the text.

2. *TV Guide* 8 (October 1988): 32.

3. Michael Barrier, "The Clay's the Thing," *Nation's Business* (December 1988): 57. Future references appear parenthetically within the text.

4. Joan Hamilton, "You've Come a Long Way Gumby," *Business Week* 8 (December 1986): 74.

5. Quoted in William L. Andrews, *The Literary Career of Charles W. Chesnutt* (Baton Rouge: Louisiana State UP, 1980) 69–70. Future references appear parenthetically within the text.

6. Quoted in Craig Werner, "The Framing of Charles W. Chesnutt: Practical Deconstruction in the Afro-American Tradition," in *Southern Literature and Literary Theory*, ed. Jefferson Humphries (Athens: U of Georgia P, 1990) 345. Future references appear parenthetically within the text.

7. Eric Selinger, "Aunts, Uncles and Audience: Gender and Genre in Charles Chesnutt's *The Conjure Woman*," *Black American Literature Forum* 25 (1991): 670.

8. Quoted in Werner 352.

9. Quoted in Andrews 45.

10. Quoted in Andrews 35.

11. Cornel West, "The Postmodern Crisis of the Black Intellectuals," in *Cultural Studies*, ed. Lawrence Grossberg, Cary Nelson, and Paula A. Treichler (New York: Routledge, 1992) 695.

12. Pamela L. Caughie, " 'Not Entirely Strange, . . . Not Entirely Friendly': *Passing* and Pedagogy," *College English* 54 (1992): 775–93.

13. Charles W. Chesnutt, *The Marrow of Tradition*, in *Three Classic African-American Novels*, ed. Henry Louis Gates, Jr. (New York: Vintage-Random, 1990) 645.

14. Quoted in Henry Louis Gates, Jr., Introduction to *Three Classic African-American Novels*, ed. Gates (New York: Vintage-Random, 1990) xvi.

15. Jean Toomer, *Cane* (1923; rpt. New York: Liveright, 1975) 8.

Chronology

1858   Charles Waddell Chesnutt born June 20 in Cleveland, son of Andrew Jackson and Ann Maria Chesnutt.

1866   The Chesnutts return to their former home in Fayetteville, North Carolina, immediately after the Civil War.

1871   Ann Maria Chesnutt dies.

1873   Charles begins teaching locally in order to help support the family.

1877   Becomes a teacher at the Colored Normal School in Fayetteville.

1878   Marries Susan Perry.

1879   Travels to Washington, D.C., in search of work; returns without a job but with renewed determination to leave the South.

1880   Takes over as principal of the Normal School.

1883   Travels to New York, where he finds work as a Dow Jones reporter and stenographer. Moves to Cleveland in the fall and begins work, first as a railroad company clerk, later as a legal stenographer.

1884   His occupational situation clarified, Chesnutt brings his family to Cleveland.

1885   Begins contributing sketches and anecdotes to humor magazines, including *Tid-Bits* and *Puck*. Publishes his first significant story, "Uncle Peter's House," in the Cleveland *News and Herald*. Undertakes legal studies.

1887   "The Goophered Grapevine" appears in the prestigious *Atlantic Monthly*. Chesnutt passes the Ohio Bar and joins the law offices of Henderson, Kline, and Tolles.

1888   Opens his own office as a court reporter. "Po' Sandy" appears in the *Atlantic Monthly*.

1889 "Dave's Neckliss," "The Conjurer's Revenge," and "The Sheriff's Children" all appear in print. Chesnutt writes the first version of "Rena Walden" and contemplates abandoning dialect fiction. "What Is a White Man?" appears in the New York *Independent*.

1891 Houghton Mifflin rejects Chesnutt's proposal for a collection of stories.

1896 Travels in Europe.

1897 Discusses the possibility of a story collection with Walter Hines Page.

1898 The *Atlantic Monthly* publishes "The Wife of His Youth."

1899 Page oversees publication of *The Conjure Woman*. Chesnutt convinces Houghton Mifflin to publish a second collection featuring his nondialect stories. *The Wife of His Youth and Other Stories of the Color Line* appears in time for the Christmas trade. Chesnutt closes his stenography business in September and begins earning his living as a writer. Small, Maynard in Boston publishes his biography of Frederick Douglass in the Beacon Series on Eminent Americans.

1900 William Dean Howells writes a glowing review of Chesnutt's stories in the *Atlantic Monthly*. "Rena Walden" appears finally as *The House Behind the Cedars*, Chesnutt's first novel. He contributes a controversial series of articles on race amalgamation, entitled "The Future American," to the Boston *Evening Transcript*.

1901 Houghton Mifflin publishes *The Marrow of Tradition*, which receives guarded reviews. Chesnutt reopens his stenography business.

1902 Turned down for membership in Cleveland's exclusive Rowfant Club.

1903 "The Disfranchisement of the Negro" appears in *The Negro Problem: A Series of Articles by Representative American Negroes of To-day*.

1904   "Baxter's Procrustes" published in the *Atlantic Monthly*. Chesnutt accepts membership on Booker T. Washington's "Committee of Twelve."

1905   Doubleday, Page publishes *The Colonel's Dream*. Chesnutt attends Mark Twain's 70th birthday party in New York City. Delivers the lecture "Race Prejudice: Its Causes and Its Cure" before the Boston Historical and Literary Association.

1910   Addresses the National Negro Committee, later the NAACP, and serves on its General Committee. Accepts membership in the Rowfant Club.

1912   "The Doll" appears in *Crisis*.

1928   Awarded the NAACP's Spingarn Medal.

1931   Publishes "Post-Bellum—Pre-Harlem" in *Colophon*.

1932   Dies on November 15.

Selected Bibliography

Primary Sources

Published Collections of Short Stories

The Conjure Woman. Boston: Houghton Mifflin, 1899; London: Gay & Bird, 1899. Includes: "The Goophered Grapevine," "Po' Sandy," "Mars Jeems's Nightmare," "The Conjurer's Revenge," "Sis' Becky's Pickaninny," "The Gray Wolf's Ha'nt," and "Hot-Foot Hannibal."

The Wife of His Youth and Other Stories of the Color Line. Boston: Houghton Mifflin, 1899. Includes: "The Wife of His Youth," "Her Virginia Mammy," "The Sheriff's Children," "A Matter of Principle," "Cicely's Dream," "The Passing of Grandison," "Uncle Wellington's Wives," "The Bouquet," and "The Web of Circumstance."

Uncollected Stories

"Appreciation." *Puck*, April 20, 1887, 128.

"Aunt Lucy's Search." *Family Fiction*, April 16, 1887.

"Aunt Mimy's Son." *Youth's Companion*, March 1, 1900, 104–5.

"A Bad Night." Atlanta *Constitution*, August 2, 1886, 5.

"Baxter's Procrustes." *Atlantic Monthly* 93 (June 1904): 823–30.

"The Bunch of Yellow Roses" [same as "The Bouquet"]. *Living Age*, April 7, 1900, 63–66.

"A Busy Day in a Lawyer's Office." *Tid-Bits*, January 15, 1887.

"Cartwright's Mistake." Cleveland *News and Herald*, September 19, 1888.

"A Cause Celebre." *Puck*, January 14, 1891, 354.

"Concerning Father." *Crisis* 37 (May 1930): 153–55.

"Dave's Neckliss." *Atlantic Monthly* 64 (October 1889): 500–508.

"A Deep Sleeper." *Two Tales*, March 11, 1893, 1–8.

"The Doctor's Wife." Chicago *Leader*, June 1, 1887.

"The Doll." *Crisis* 3 (April 1912): 248–52.

"A Doubtful Success." Cleveland *News and Herald*, February 17, 1888.

"An Eloquent Appeal." *Puck*, June 6, 1888, 246.

"The Fall of Adam." *Family Fiction*, December 25, 1886.

"A Fatal Restriction." *Puck*, May 1, 1889, 166.

"A Fool's Paradise." *Family Fiction*, November 24, 1888.

"A Grass Widow." *Family Fiction,* May 14, 1887.
"Gratitude." *Puck,* December 28, 1888, 300.
"How a Good Man Went Wrong." *Puck,* November 28, 1888, 214.
"How Dasdy Came Through." *Family Fiction,* February 12, 1887.
"Lonesome Ben." *Southern Workman* 29 (March 1900): 137–45.
"McDugald's Mule." *Family Fiction,* January 15, 1887.
"The March of Progress." *Century* 61 (January 1901): 422–28.
"The Marked Tree." *Crisis* 29 (December–January 1924–25): 59–64, 110–13.
"A Metropolitan Experience." Chicago *Ledger,* June 15, 1887.
"A Midnight Adventure." New Haven *Register,* December 6, 1887.
"Mr. Taylor's Funeral." *Crisis* 9–10 (April–May 1915): 313–16, 34–37.
"The Original of the Hatchet Story." *Puck,* April 24, 1889, 132.
"The Partners." *Southern Workman* 30 (May 1901): 271–78.
"The Prophet Peter." *Hathaway-Brown Magazine,* April 1, 1906, 51–66.
"A Roman Antique." *Puck,* July 17, 1889, 351.
"A Secret Ally." New Haven *Register,* December 6, 1886.
"She Reminded Him." *Puck,* September 21, 1887, 58.
"A Soulless Corporation." *Tid-Bits,* April 16, 1887.
"The Sway-Backed House." *Outlook* 66 (November 1900): 588–93.
"A Tight Boot." Cleveland *News and Herald,* January 30, 1886.
"Tobe's Tribulations." *Southern Workman* 29 (November 1900): 656–64.
"Tom's Warm Welcome." *Family Fiction,* November 27, 1886.
"Uncle Peter's House." Cleveland *News and Herald,* December, 1885.
"A Victim of Heredity; or, Why the Darkey Loves Chicken." *Self-Culture Magazine* 11 (July 1900): 404–9.
"A Virginia Chicken." *Household Realm,* August, 1887.
"Wine and Water." *Family Fiction,* April 23, 1887.

Works in Other Literary Genres

NOVELS

The Colonel's Dream. New York: Doubleday Page, 1905; London: A. Constable, 1905.
The House Behind the Cedars. Boston: Houghton Mifflin, 1900.
The Marrow of Tradition. Boston: Houghton Mifflin, 1901.

POEMS

"The Ballad of Fair Oscar." *Tid-Bits,* December 18, 1886.
"A Battle Hymn." *Social Circle Journal* 18 (October 1886): 1.
"A Father's Dream." Cleveland *Voice,* March 8, 1885.
"A Summer Cloud." Cleveland *Voice,* August 30, 1885.
"To the Grand Army of the Republic." Cleveland *Leader,* September 8, 1901.

Nonfiction

"Abraham Lincoln: An Appreciation." *Southwestern Christian Advocate* 43 (February 1909): 1, 8.
"A Defamer of His Race." *Critic* 38 (April 1901): 350–51.
"The Disfranchisement of the Negro," in *The Negro Problem: A Series of Articles by Representative American Negroes of To-day*. New York: James Pott, 1903, 79–124.
Frederick Douglass. Boston: Small Maynard, 1899; London: Kegan Paul, 1899.
"The Free Colored People of North Carolina." *Southern Workman* 31 (March 1902): 136–41.
"The Future American: A Complete Race-Amalgamation Likely to Occur." Boston *Evening Transcript*, September 1, 1900, 24.
"The Future American: A Stream of Dark Blood in the Veins of Southern Whites." Boston *Evening Transcript*, August 25, 1900, 15.
"The Future American: What the Race Is Likely to Become in the Process of Time." Boston *Evening Transcript*, August 18, 1900, 20.
"The Mission of the Drama." *Cygnet* 1 (1920): 11–12.
"A Multitude of Counselors." New York *Independent*, April 2, 1891, 4–5.
"The Negro in Art." *Crisis* 33 (November 1926): 28–29.
"The Negro in Cleveland." *Clevelander* 5 (1930): 3–4.
"The Negro Franchise." Boston *Evening Transcript*, May 11, 1901, 18.
"Obliterating the Color Line." Cleveland *World*, October 23, 1901, 4.
"On the Future of His People." *Saturday Evening Post*, January 10, 1900, 646.
"Peonage, Or the New Slavery." *Voice of the Negro* 1 (September 1904): 394–97.
"A Plea for the American Negro." *Critic* 36 (February 1900): 160–61.
"Post-Bellum—Pre-Harlem." *Colophon* 2, no. 5 (1931); rpt. *Crisis* 40 (June 1931): 193–94.
"Race Ideals and Examples." *A.M.E. Review* 30 (1913): 101–17.
"Race Prejudice: Its Causes and Its Cures." *Alexander's Magazine* 1 (July 1905): 21–26.
"Superstition and Folklore of the South." *Modern Culture* 13 (May 1901): 231–35.
"A Visit to Tuskegee." Cleveland *Leader*, March 31, 1901, 19.
"What Is a White Man?" New York *Independent*, May 30, 1889, 5–6.
"The White and the Black." Boston *Evening Transcript*, March 20, 1901, 13.

Secondary Sources

Books

Andrews, William L. *The Literary Career of Charles W. Chesnutt*. Baton Rouge: Louisiana State Univ. Press, 1980.

Baker, Houston A. *Modernism and the Harlem Renaissance*. Chicago: Univ. of Chicago Press, 1987.

Bone, Robert. *Down Home: Origins of the Afro-American Short Story*. New York: Columbia Univ. Press, 1975.

Brawley, Benjamin. *The Negro in American Literature and Art*. New York: Duffield, 1910.

Brodhead, Richard H. *Cultures of Letters: Scenes of Reading and Writing in Nineteenth Century America*. Chicago: Univ. of Chicago Press, 1993.

Chesnutt, Helen M. *Charles Waddell Chesnutt: Pioneer of the Color Line*. Chapel Hill: Univ. of North Carolina Press, 1952.

Heermance, J. Noel. *Charles Waddell Chesnutt: America's First Great Black Novelist*. Hamden, Conn.: Archon, 1974.

Keller, Frances Richardson. *An American Crusade: The Life of Charles Waddell Chesnutt*. Provo: Brigham Young Univ. Press, 1978.

Mackethan, Lucinda Hardwick. *The Dream of Arcady: Place and Time in Southern Literature*. Baton Rouge: Louisiana State Univ. Press, 1980.

Pickens, Ernestine Williams. *Charles W. Chesnutt and the Progressive Movement*. New York: Pace Univ. Press, 1994.

Redding, J. Saunders. *To Make a Poet Black*. Chapel Hill: Univ. of North Carolina Press, 1939.

Render, Sylvia Lyons. *Charles W. Chesnutt*. Boston: Twayne, 1980.

———. *The Short Fiction of Charles W. Chesnutt*. Washington, D.C.: Howard Univ. Press, 1974.

Sollors, Werner. *Beyond Ethnicity: Consent and Descent in American Culture*. New York: Oxford Univ. Press, 1986.

Sundquist, Eric J. *To Wake the Nations: Race in the Making of American Literature*. Cambridge: Harvard Univ. Press, 1993.

Articles and Reviews

Andrews, William L. "The Significance of Charles W. Chesnutt's 'Conjure Stories.'" *Southern Literary Journal* 7 (1974): 78–99.

———. "William Dean Howells and Charles W. Chesnutt: Criticism and Race Fiction in the Age of Booker T. Washington." *American Literature* 48 (1976): 327–39.

Babb, Valerie. "Subversion and Repatriation in *The Conjure Woman*." *Southern Quarterly* 25 (Winter 1987): 66–75.

Baldwin, Richard. "The Art of *The Conjure Woman*." *American Literature* 43 (1971): 383–98.

Braithwaite, William Stanley. "The Negro in American Literature," in *The New Negro*, ed. Alain Locke. New York: Albert and Charles Boni, 1925.

Britt, David D. "Chesnutt's Conjure Tales: What You See Is What You Get." *CLA Journal* 15 (1972): 269–83.

Brodhead, Richard H. Introduction to *The Conjure Woman and Other Conjure Tales,* ed. Richard H. Brodhead. Durham: Duke Univ. Press, 1993.

————. Introduction to *The Journals of Charles W. Chesnutt,* ed. Richard H. Brodhead. Durham: Duke Univ. Press, 1993.

Dixon, Melvin. "The Teller as Folk Trickster in Chesnutt's *The Conjure Woman.*" *CLA Journal* 18 (1974): 186–97.

Elder, Arlene A. "Chesnutt on Washington: An Essential Ambivalence." *Phylon* 38 (1977): 1–8.

Farwell, Julia B. "Goophering Around: Authority and the Trick of Storytelling in Charles W. Chesnutt's *The Conjure Woman,*" in *Tricksterism in Turn of the Century American Literature: A Multi-Cultural Perspective,* ed. Elizabeth Ammons. Hanover, N.H.: Univ. Press of New England, 1994, 79–92.

Fienberg, Lorne. "Charles W. Chesnutt and Uncle Julius: Black Storytellers at the Crossroads." *Studies in American Fiction* 15 (1987): 161–73.

Ferguson, Sally Ann. "Chesnutt's 'The Conjurer's Revenge': The Economics of Direct Confrontation." *Obsidian* 7 (1981): 37–42.

Hemenway, Robert. " 'Baxter's Procrustes': Irony and Protest." *CLA Journal* 18 (1974): 172–85.

————. "The Functions of Folklore in Charles Chesnutt's *The Conjure Woman.*" *Journal of the Folklore Institute* 13 (1976): 283–309.

Hovet, Theodore R. "Chesnutt's 'The Goophered Grapevine' as Social Criticism." *Negro American Literature Forum* 7 (1973): 83–85.

Hurd, Myles Raymond. "Booker T., Blacks, and Brogues: Chesnutt's Sociohistorical Links to Realism in 'Uncle Wellington's Wives.' " *American Literary Realism* 26 (Winter 1994): 19–29.

Kinnamon, Ken. "Three Black Writers and the Anthologized Canon," in *American Realism and the Canon,* ed. Tom Quirk and Gary Scharnhorst. Newark: Univ. of Delaware Press, 1994, 143–53.

Lauter, Paul. "The Literatures of America: A Comparative Discipline," in *Redefining American Literary History,* ed. A. LaVonne Brown Ruoff and Jerry W. Ward. New York: Modern Language Association, 1990, 9–34.

Molyneux, Sandra. "Expanding the Collective Memory: Charles W. Chesnutt's Conjure Woman Tales," in *Memory, Narrative and Identity: New Essays in Ethnic American Literatures,* ed. Amritjit Singh, Joseph T. Skerrett Jr., and Robert E. Hogan. Boston: Northeastern Univ. Press, 1994, 164–78.

Nowatzki, Robert. "Passing in a White Genre: Charles W. Chesnutt's Negation of the Plantation Tradition in *The Conjure Woman.*" *American Literary Realism* 27 (1995): 20–36.

Patton, Richard J. "Studyin' 'Bout Ole Julius: A Note on Charles W. Chesnutt's Uncle Julius McAdoo." *American Literary Realism* 24 (1992): 72–79.

Selinger, Eric. "Aunts, Uncles, Audience: Gender and Genre in Charles Chesnutt's *The Conjure Woman.*" *Black American Literature Forum* 25 (1991): 665–88.

Slote, Ben. "Listening to 'The Goophered Grapevine' and Hearing Raisins Sing." *American Literary History* 6 (Winter 1994): 684–94.

Sollors, Werner. "The Goopher in Charles Chesnutt's Conjure Tales: Superstition, Ethnicity, and Modern Metamorphosis." *Letterature d'America* 6 (1986): 107–29.

Stepto, Robert B. " 'The Simple but Intensely Human Inner Life of Slavery': Storytelling and the Revision of History in Charles W. Chesnutt's 'Uncle Julius Stories,' " in *History and Tradition in Afro-American Culture,* ed. Gunter H. Lenz. Frankfurt: Campus, 1984, 29–55.

Terry, Eugene. "The Shadow of Slavery in Charles Chesnutt's *The Conjure Woman.*" *Ethnic Groups* 4 (1982): 104–25.

Walcott, Ronald. "Chesnutt's 'The Sheriff's Children' as Parable." *Negro American Literature Forum* 7 (1973): 86–88.

Werner, Craig. "The Framing of Charles W. Chesnutt: Practical Deconstruction in the Afro-American Tradition," in *Southern Literature and Literary Theory,* ed. Jefferson Humphries. Athens: Univ. of Georgia Press, 1990, 339–65.

White, Jeannette S. "Bearing Slavery's Darkest Secrets: Charles Chesnutt's Conjure Tales as Masks of Truth." *Southern Literary Journal* 27 (Fall 1994): 85–103.

Wideman, John Edgar. "Charles Chesnutt and the WPA Narratives: The Oral and Literate in Afro-American Literature," in *The Slave's Narrative,* ed. Charles T. Davis and Henry Louis Gates Jr. New York: Oxford Univ. Press, 1985, 59–78.

Bibliographies

Andrews, William L. "Charles Waddell Chesnutt: An Essay in Bibliography." *Resources for American Literary Study* 6 (Spring 1976): 3–22.

Ellison, Curtis W., and E. W. Metcalf Jr. *Charles W. Chesnutt: A Reference Guide.* Boston: G. K. Hall, 1977.

Index

165

The Author

Henry B. Wonham is the author of *Mark Twain and the Art of the Tall Tale* (Oxford, 1993) and editor of *Criticism and the Color Line: Desegregating American Literary Studies* (Rutgers, 1996). He teaches American literature at the University of Oregon.

The Editors

Gary Scharnhorst is professor of English at the University of New Mexico, coeditor of *American Literary Realism*, and editor in alternating years of *American Literary Scholarship: An Annual*. He is the author or editor of books about Horatio Alger Jr., Charlotte Perkins Gilman, Bret Harte, Nathaniel Hawthorne, Henry David Thoreau, and Mark Twain, and he has taught in Germany on Fulbright fellowships three times (1978–1979, 1985–1986, 1993). He is also the current president of the Western Literature Association and the Pacific Northwest American Studies Association.

Eric Haralson is assistant professor of English at the State University of New York at Stony Brook. He has published articles on American and English literature—in *American Literature, Nineteenth-Century Literature,* the *Arizona Quarterly, American Literary Realism,* and the *Henry James Review,* as well as in several essay collections. He is also the editor of *The Garland Encyclopedia of American Nineteenth-Century Poetry.*